CHATS ON OLD COINS

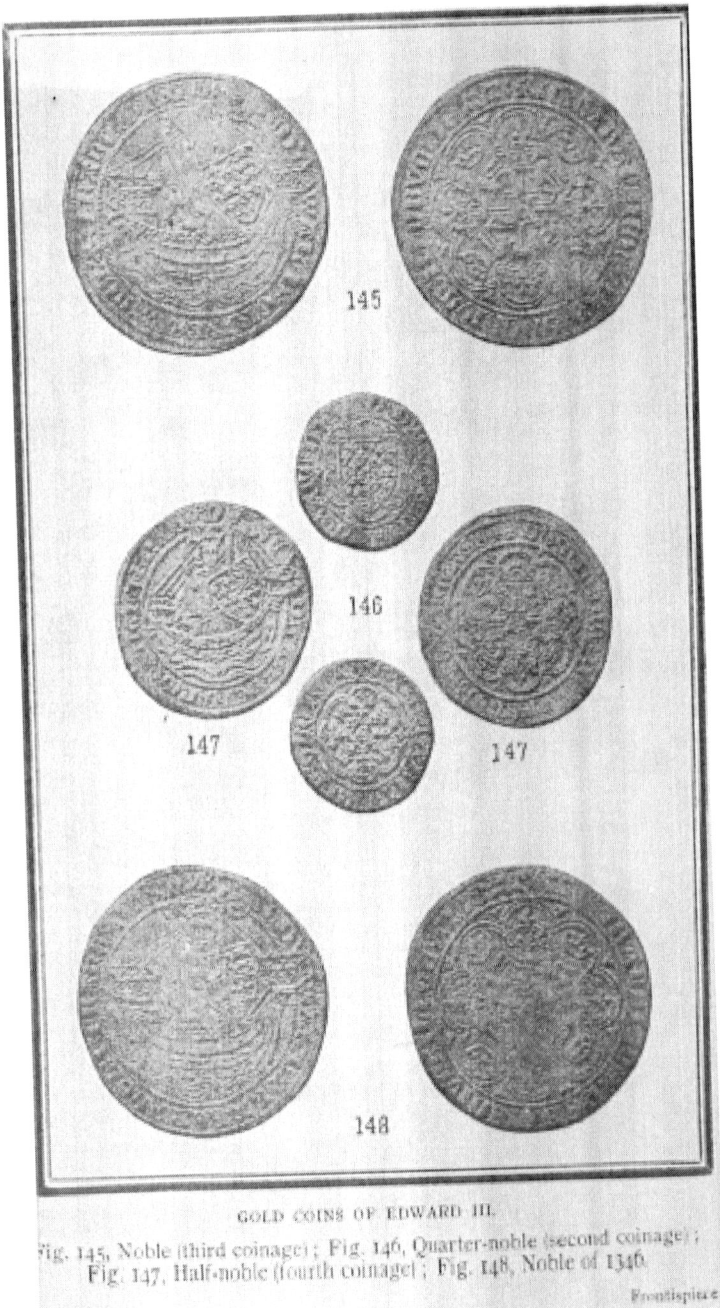

GOLD COINS OF EDWARD III.

Fig. 145, Noble (third coinage); Fig. 146, Quarter-noble (second coinage); Fig. 147, Half-noble (fourth coinage); Fig. 148, Noble of 1346.

Frontispiece

CHATS ON OLD COINS

FRED W. BURGESS

WITH 258 ILLUSTRATIONS

GYAN

Published by

Gyan Publishing House
5, Ansari Road
Daryaganj, New Delhi-110002
Phone: 011-47034999, 9811692060
E-mail: books@gyanbooks.com

Distribution Network
gyanbooks.com
India, USA, Canada, UK, Australia, France

ISBN : 978-81-212-3229-6 (PB)
First Published, London, 1913

2nd Impression 2020

Printed at: Gyan Press, Delhi.

Chats on Old Coins
Author: Fred W. Burgess

CHATS ON OLD COINS

BY

FRED. W. BURGESS

WITH 258 ILLUSTRATIONS

LONDON

T. FISHER UNWIN

ADELPHI TERRACE

PREFACE

NUMISMATIC literature has hitherto been prepared for the specialist, and adapted to those who wish to possess in categorical form a complete—or as nearly so as the writer's knowledge enabled him to make it—list of the coins and medals of the period under review. Some books have been written for the beginner and those who at small cost were desirous of obtaining an elementary account of the particular branch of coin collecting in which they were interested. Few attempts, however, have been made to provide in condensed form a book dealing with the obsolete currencies which have, throughout the world's history, been used by its most prominent nations.

In this little work the author has endeavoured to "skim the cream" off the heavier and, to some, drier problems of numismatology, and to present in acceptable "popular" form the more interesting facts which should be known to every collector.

Among the branches of study touched upon are those associated with the coins of the ancients most prominent in European history. The beauties of Greek coins and Roman medallions are strongly in evidence. The dawn of civilization as seen in the early currency of Britain is pointed out, and step by step the story of the coinage of Great Britain and her dependencies—the Greater Britain beyond the Seas—is unfolded.

Recognizing not only that the blood-relationship of the freeborn sons of American soil makes the coinage of the Old World which their forefathers handled interesting to them, but that the coins used by dwellers in the United States and in Canada are valued by English collectors, I have given prominence to American currencies.

The British regal coinage has so frequently been supplemented by token issues, which have for a time become a part of the national currency, that I have included in "Chats on Old Coins" a few chapters on tokens.

As an old collector of many years' standing, I have at different times specialized on nearly all the branches of numismatic research referred to; and I believe there are many others, too, who are interested in the study of coins and tokens from the broader standpoint of the coinage of Greece,

Rome, and all English-speaking nations, to whom such a book as I have aimed at providing will be welcome.

The illustrations, which are very representative, should be helpful to many. They are numerous, and cover a wide field. Many of them are illustrative of pieces in my own collections, and others have been secured by the courtesy of collectors to whom my thanks are due.

I wish to acknowledge the kindness of the Keeper of Coins at the British Museum for giving me facilities in illustrating some of the coins in the national collection. I would also place on record my indebtedness to Messrs. Sotheby, Wilkinson & Hodge, who have allowed me to reproduce illustrations of many fine coins which have passed through their hands.

The illustrations of tokens are from a fine collection formed nearly one hundred years ago, and were then carefully engraved.

If my efforts to convey useful and "chatty" information on the several branches of collecting outlined encourage any of my readers to go deeper into the fascinating hobby of collecting coins which teach history, I shall be more than satisfied.

FRED. W. BURGESS.

LONDON, 1913.

CONTENTS

ILLUSTRATIONS

GREEK.

ROMAN.

SAXON.

ENGLISH.

ENGLISH.

BRITISH COLONIAL.

ISLE OF MAN AND CHANNEL ISLANDS.

IRISH AND SCOTCH.

I

THE COLLECTOR'S AIM

CHAPTER I

THE COLLECTOR'S AIM

An outline of the hobby—The chief aims of the collector—Marks of origin—The nomenclature of coins.

COLLECTORS' hobbies for the most part take the form of hoarding things which to the uninitiated are little understood and rarely appreciated. The science of numismatics, on the contrary, although dealing with rarities, is chiefly concerned with familiar objects, for coins of the realm, in greater or lesser quantities, are to be found in the possession of every one. It has been so for ages, for ever since primitive barter was supplanted by the more convenient use of a coined medium of exchange, of some definite value, the peoples of all civilized nations have daily handled current coin. Curiously enough, like many common objects, gold, silver, or bronze paid away is scarcely noted, and a passing glance suffices to determine its relative worth or buying power. Thus it is that the absence of a denominational mark is unnoticed, and even a coin rubbed almost smooth causes its owner little or no inconvenience.

In the days when those who used money had none of the educational advantages of the present day, there was greater international use of coins, and as long as it was of the same metal and approximately of similar size almost any coin or token passed current. This, probably, accounts for the curious mixture of coins found in buried or concealed hoards. Indeed, until quite recent times traders' tills contained a varied assortment of pieces they had taken at the rate of the standard coin of nearest size in the country in which they lived.

The study of numismatics reveals many fields of research, especially so the earlier issues of nations with a "history," and chiefly is this the case with the coins of Ancient Rome so closely associated with Britain. Old coins illustrate events which would otherwise have been forgotten; they have a bearing on the faiths of the people living at the time they were issued, and are scarcely less valuable to students of the customs and habits of those who governed conquered nations. As a science numismatics is closely allied to art, for sculpture, drawing, and design are all shown in the work of the die-sinker which has been handed down to us on well-authenticated specimens.

When a collector takes up a new hobby, or determines to give more attention to one in which he has lost interest, he naturally turns to those examples he already possesses. It is frequently this nucleus that determines the bent of the specialist—for sooner or later a true collector who takes a genuine interest in his hobby becomes an enthusiast, and an enthusiast, if he has concentration and a studious mind, becomes a specialist. He gradually acquires knowledge, and by applying it secures better specimens; for he is soon discontented with inferior ones. The desire to make his collection representative is accentuated whenever he obtains some greater treasure than he has hitherto possessed.

Perfection is the laudable aim of the advanced collector. The admirer of ceramics appreciates the perfect specimen, and avoids cracked cups and saucers; the philatelist craves for stamps with original gum and freak watermarks; and so the numismatist seeks perfection in mint condition. It may be pointed out that the true coin is one issued by a duly appointed authority. It must be the currency of the country, district, or town in which it circulates, and have a legal and accepted value, in that it differs from token currency which is a pledge, usually redeemable in current coin by the issuer. Such tokens, however, in the past have been freely circulated, and under exceptional conditions have been accepted without dispute as the local currency; and they have even become incorporated in the national coinage of this and other countries.

The collection of coins is no new thing, for many of the finds of ancient coins have been so varied in the reigns included in them that it would seem highly probable that they were gathered together from a collector's view point. Others have stored up coins in mint condition on account of their beauty or rarity, or from the peculiar circumstances under which they were issued, and have handed them on in almost mint condition. Many fine cabinets have been got together as the result of patient research, often to come under the hammer in a few years' time. Such private collections are, alas! rarely open to the public view; fortunately, however, many museums contain fairly representative collections, and the unrivalled national collection in the British Museum is available.

Reference has been made to the mint bloom so much desired by the collector. This term is somewhat elastic, in that if applied to coins recently minted it means that the fresh bloom of the mint must be untarnished, and the face of the coin without scratch; whereas the same state of perfection in a coin of Ancient Greece is well-nigh unobtainable, and therefore the term must be one of relative meaning, understood by experts somewhat differently in connection with various mintages.

The ambition of many quite early in their numismatic careers is to catalogue their cabinets; but to make such a list intelligible, or to understand what is written by experts in reference to coins, it is necessary to know the terms and accepted abbreviations in common use. Briefly, for the benefit of amateurs, some of the chief terms relating to the particular branches of coin collecting mentioned in the following chapters are here given.

Obviously marks of origin should receive attention first, in that to locate the coin to its proper country is of primary importance; to determine its age and fix the reign during which it was minted follows in proper sequence; and then, if possible, to add the year and place of mintage, which should enable the collector to assign it to the right place in the cabinet. Some ancient coins were uninscribed; others bore the name of the country of issue in abbreviated form. The name of the Emperor or Governor by whose orders they were struck was inscribed upon the coins of Imperial Rome, the legends upon the pieces generally adding some explanatory particulars, mostly abbreviated. The coins of Great Britain, however, are more easily recognized, in that the country as well as the name of the king, is inscribed thereon. The exact date of Roman coins can often be told from the event the coin is intended to commemorate, by its inscription or type, and also from the title of the ruler, or from the year of his Consulate or Tributian power. The place of mintage was added to some of the coins of Rome, and it is generally seen on the Saxon and Anglo-Norman issues. In later years English coins have had upon them certain mint marks denoting the places where they were struck; and the name of the moneyer, mint-master, and, more recently, the initials of the die-sinker have been added. It will thus be seen that there is much to be learned from mint marks, and that they have a bearing on the value of a rare coin. To a certain extent there is an affinity between heraldry and such marks, which often took their forms from the crests or armorial bearings of those who were responsible for their issue.

The most important marks of recent days are

crosses, of which there are several varieties. There is the cross *patonce*, which is said to resemble in the points of the terminals a cross-hilted dagger. There is a *crosslet*, the ends of which are crosses near the extremities; the cross *voided* has the inner portion blank, and the cross *pierced* has the mark of a little hole in the centre. The cross *Calvary* finds its base on one or more steps. The *pall* mint mark is very much like the letter Y, and is usually found on Episcopal coins, the word itself being a contraction of *pallium*. The *pheon* is a mint mark chiefly found on Tudor coins, and is said to be equivalent to the broad arrow of to-day. The *fleur-de-lis* is often seen, and of course it figures on the arms of the earlier English Sovereigns, who quartered France with England. The *annulet* is a plain ring; the *mullet* is in reality the wheel of a spur. The *martlet* is a bird of the marten type; and the *gerb*, a sheaf of wheat, three of which form the arms of Chester, is a mark found on coins minted there. The escallop shell, acorn, rose, lion, crescent, and key may be mentioned as other common mint marks.

As an instance of marks of origin, denoting the origin of the metal and not of the place of mintage, there is the name "Lima," under the bust of George II, seen on many of his coins of silver and gold. This is explainable in that Lima is the capital of Peru, which was a Spanish possession in 1739, when this country was at war with Spain. It was near Lima that the British fleet took a Spanish treasure ship, in which was no less than £300,000 worth of gold and silver. Admiral Anson, who brought the treasure to port, was made a peer, and the metal used at the mint in British coinage received the impress "Lima."

Under the bust on coins of Queen Anne, mostly dated 1702 and 1703, is the place-name "Vigo." In the first-named year Sir George Rooke attacked the French and Spanish fleets in the port of Vigo, and there captured much bullion and plate, which eventually found its way to the Royal Mint. An instance of coins owing their names to the places from which the metal of mintage came is that of the guinea, which had formerly been called a sovereign. The coins, minted from gold which came from the coast of Guinea, brought chiefly by the African Company, were so named. The East India Company furnished our mint with some gold, a service acknowledged by the letters E.I.C. below the bust of George II on most of the gold coins of his reign.

Many of the coins of ancient nations are remarkable for their purity of metal. The English currency of gold and silver, and copper, too, has with a few fortunate exceptions been well maintained in all regal issues. Coins have been cast, struck, hammered, milled, and minted by intricate machines during their evolution from a lump of metal. The thinness of the hammered silver of the Middle Ages made it very easy for fraudulent persons to clip. The first serious attempt to prevent this fraud was made by Oliver Cromwell, who introduced edge inscriptions. The date letters and marks of ancient coins fell into disuse, and the practice of dating them was only revived in comparatively recent times, and consequently young collectors, unfamiliar with the legends, frequently abbreviated, in Greek or Latin, peculiar to certain periods, are apt to place their specimens in a wrong category. Queen Mary was the first English Sovereign to date her coinage, which she did in 1553, using Roman numerals. From that time onwards there is not much trouble in fixing the reign and the year of issue of English coins. Some difficulty is experienced, however, in deciding upon their original current values, in that most of the old pieces, although thinner, were larger than current coins of the same denomination.

Marks of value were first used in the reign of Edward VI, on whose coins will be noticed "XII" for twelve pence, the mark of value being placed on the side of the king's head on the obverse. The first year of that denominated coinage was 1551. James I in a similar way marked his rose-ryal "XXX" for thirty shillings, and his spur-ryal "XV" for fifteen shillings.

The names of coins reviewed in the following chapters should be noted carefully in that they are an interesting study. In the form in which they were used they frequently present little idea of the origin of their nomenclature, the discovery of which often illuminates the purpose of their issue, and indicates the reason for the changes which were from time to time made in the currency of the nations. Especially interesting is it to trace the birth of a new coin and its gradual use in many countries. The gold stater of Philip of Macedon was not only universally employed by traders of all nations, but it gave the size and even design to others in years to come. The Roman denarius became the penny of England and Gaul. The Spanish dollar furnished the standard of currency for the New World, and countermarked or reminted became a part of our own coinage. Names of men and peoples change, so do those of coins. The "ryal" of early English sovereigns was originally called "royal," because the king was represented upon it in his royal robes of state. The sovereign of to-day comes to us from the beautiful golden coins of Tudor days, when the king was pictured as seated on his throne, holding in his hands the emblems of sovereignty. The noble, the coin instituted by Edward III, was truly a noble piece.

Notwithstanding that in the evolution of coins of many nations well-established standards of size, weight, and purity have been maintained, there have been many changes and irregularities which have their bearing on determining their correct classification.

With very few exceptions coins have, except in the earliest archaic issues, always been impressed on both sides; they are also for the most part of true coin shape—that is, circular. The principal side, or obverse, is that on which the Sovereign's head or chief emblem of the issuing country is shown. The opposite side, or reverse, frequently shows the arms or emblems of the State, or the type chosen for that special piece to distinguish it from others: it is sometimes occupied by the value of the piece, or less frequently by the name of the country. The inscription is usually round the head or emblems; the plain part not occupied by the chief devices is the field. The edge, which in modern coins is either milled, plain, or inscribed, is found in the thickness of the piece. The preservation of specimens as well as their classification being of paramount importance, it is very desirable that the collector should lose no time in providing a suitable cabinet or receptacle for his treasures, where they may retain their condition unaffected by time. The metals of currency are varied, but chiefly consist of gold, silver, and copper or bronze. To these standard metals must be added brass, pewter, aluminium, nickel, and various alloys which have been introduced from time to time experimentally.

II

THE STORY OF COINAGE

CHAPTER II

THE STORY OF COINAGE

The early adoption of currency—The spread of coined money—Method of coinage in olden time—The establishment of mints—Present-day systems.

THE most ancient form of trading was by barter, which we find described as "an exchange in kind." Such trading naturally involved disputes and "barter," in that the goods offered for commodities needed would not always have an accepted value, neither would they be appreciated in the same way. Moreover, barter was soon found to be inconvenient, and we find nearly all the early nations at the very dawn of their civilization making use of some recognized mediums by which goods could be appraised and cattle and other things sold or partly exchanged. The primitive nations still in their Stone Age have their own systems, and although the medium may seem of small value to us it is the standard by which their wealth and their requirements are gauged, and therefore sufficient for their purpose. With some this medium is found in beads, bangles, shells, and in trinkets of small intrinsic value as assessed by our standard. With the more advanced there is real and substantial value in the skins of wild beasts and tusks of ivory offered by the hunter, and in the precious stones and mineral treasures of those who have found out some of the secrets of Nature's store-house.

Metal was early assigned a prominent place in the monetary standard. Barbarian and savage used it, and the nations of antiquity soon began to tale and weigh bars of the precious metal, and to give them an acknowledged value. The wealth of pastoral peoples lay in their herds and cattle; the value they put upon an ox became the worth of the standard medium, and when the Romans coined money it took its name from the cattle with which the farmers had been wont to buy other commodities. Money is described by an authority on such things as "that which is among the barbarous nations for effecting exchanges of property, and in the terms of which values are reckoned, as, sheep, wampum, copper rings, quills of salt, gold dust, shovel blades, or other much-used staples, is in common language their money." The ring moneys of the early Celtic tribes found in Ireland have their counterpart in other parts of the world. The nations of the Far East, with their older civilizations, show in the forms of their "coins" the evolution from the actual article employed in barter to an accepted currency. The spade-shaped pieces of brass and knife-money of the Chinese tell of tools and weapons in existence before coins. Cowrie-shells were used throughout the Eastern islands and on the borders of the coast. Snail-money comes from Burma, and fish-hook money from the Malay Peninsular. The Greeks used ingots of brass, and the Jews employed shekels—weights, not coined money.

In European Greece Phidon, King of the Argos, is said to have been so impressed with the value of the invention of the Lydians, who had then begun to mark their bars or ingots with a punch on which was a distinctive mark, that he followed suit, and to inaugurate the new departure sent a number of the bars of metal which had hitherto served the purpose of a medium for the transaction of trade to the Temple of Hera at Argos. Such centres of commerce as Athens and Corinth soon followed. The small bars of metal used in Ancient Greece were spiked, and not unlike an obelisk, hence the name of an early coin, the obolus—six of such pieces could be held in the hand, thus *drachma*, a handful, became the name of the standard coin of early days. Then came the more convenient bean-shaped pieces impressed with a punch, which a few years later might have been seen commonly used among the trading communities of Europe and Asia.

The method of coinage of these first mints was simple and yet effective. The oval-shaped ingots, or flans, were stamped on one side only; the reverse, however, bore the incuse mark of the second stamp or die upon which the ingot had been placed to make the impress of the obverse. This punch mark early gave the die-sinkers the idea of a second die, thus producing a double-marked coin. At that time the devices were exceedingly crude, merely a portion of some animal, a bull preferably. The distinguishing marks had as yet to come; they were not long in making their appearance, for the value and importance of denoting the origin of the coins was soon apparent.

With the spread of the use of such pieces it is obvious that the coining of money could not be other than in the hands of some accredited authority, which in the European islands of the Mediterranean was centralized within each one or in each group; on the mainland mints were soon set up, and properly appointed mint-masters and die-sinkers caused improvements to be effected as time went on. Perhaps the spirit of commercial competition had already been awakened. Who can tell?

It may be convenient here to point out that the primitive method of striking coins was preserved for many centuries; indeed, until quite modern times. The pellet of metal assumed a circular form it is true, but until the adoption of the mill and screw in the days of Queen Elizabeth coins were hammered; the anvil and the hammer symbolically, if not actually, were the tools by which money was made.

Mints were at one time quite common, and were not, as now, confined to one or two centralized establishments where intricate machinery carries on the plan of coinage with absolute accuracy, and the most delicate instruments test and pass or reject every coin tendered. The collector owes many of his rarest curiosities to the inefficient appliances used in the past, and finds many of his "freaks" and rarities in the mistakes which those early mintmasters allowed to escape their notice.

In ancient countries towns and cities furnished their own supply of coins for local trade. The authority of those entrusted with the minting of money in the Roman Empire stretched to its uttermost parts, where were the armies of the Empire encamped. The mintmasters went with the soldiers, and took care that the troops were paid with the coins of silver and brass which they often minted from locally-mined supplies. The Saxon mints were numerous, as will be seen from a perusal of this work; in like manner Norman and even later English Sovereigns, who retained the right to strike money, set up mints at many places; the metal, anvil, and pair of dies, manipulated by hand and struck with a hammer, soon turned the flan of metal into a coin. In accounts of the London Mint, always the chief British mint of modern times, some interesting facts are recorded. In the museum of the Mint may be seen many of the early minting tools, and there also are stored a large number of old dies, some from which it looks temptingly easy to duplicate what are now among the greatest rarities of coins! The visitor to the Mint will be familiar with the splendid apparatus with which the coins of this country and of many of our colonies are now minted, and will note the marvellous progress made in the making of coins since the days of George II, when a simple screw press was used.

Gold is the standard of our present monetary system, and the country's wealth is represented by the bullion stored in the Bank of England and deposited in the large banking houses of this and other countries—in so far as money of sterling value is concerned. The bars of gold are minted and the silver is struck with its denominational accredited values, as it is required. It was not always so, for traders and others had in the past often to resort to token currencies with which to carry on the nation's trade. Sometimes the supply of bullion ran low, at others it was lack of appreciation of the growing commerce of the "nation of shopkeepers." It may occur to some that the difficulties of obtaining a supply of metal must have been great before the days of improved transport. In Saxon days silver was mined in Cornwall as it had been in Roman times. It is said that Edward I was able to get 704 lb. weight of silver from a mine in Devonshire in one year. Even until the time of George I Welsh and other native mines supplied all the silver and copper needed. There were many mines worked in Wales and Anglesey in the eighteenth century, and their owners issued tokens in the same metal for the payment of their workpeople. Peru and Mexico sent us silver and gold, and during our wars with Spain we helped ourselves to the supplies of the silver in Spanish merchant vessels on the high seas. On the day on which the eldest son of George III was born there arrived in London twenty wagon-loads of silver, landed from H.M.S. *Hermione*, taken from the Spanish. In 1842 sixty-five tons of silver arrived from China, being the amount of the ransom paid by that country. The bullion now comes from other sources, although war indemnities in bullion are received still.

III

COINS OF ANCIENT GREECE

CHAPTER III

COINS OF ANCIENT GREECE

An increasingly popular series—Local currencies—Well-defined periods—Selected examples.

THE popularity of Greek coins has been steadily growing for some years past. Their collection is no longer the exclusive hobby of wealthy men, nor is it confined to those learned in dead languages. It is now realized that it is possible to find pleasurable delight in the study of the commoner and less expensive types which were issued in large numbers in the cities of Ancient Greece, and the islands where Greek colonies were planted.

Whilst it is true rare varieties and the finest condition specimens command high prices, there are many really good coins in gold, silver, and bronze which are procurable for a moderate outlay. The value and interest of a collection grows as it becomes more representative; and although Greek issues do not take such a prominent place in numismatic research as Roman coins or those of Great Britain and her Colonies, they present many attractions to the student of ancient history. Fortunately, although the inscriptions are in ancient Greek and archaic characters, they are simple, and often consist only of the names of the places of issue. An attribute of the deity favoured there, or an emblem of the town or island, helps to fix the locality of issue.

In the later coins, from Alexander the Great onward to the foundation of Imperial Rome, ending with the coins bearing the effigy of Cleopatra, an almost unbroken series of portraits of the kings of Magna Græcia may be collected. The Greek aspect of the old gods, not always coinciding with that held by other nations, can be traced on the coins, and the differences between the views of the people of the Grecian sphere of influence and that of the Roman, which followed after, can be noted.

The splendid series of Greek coins and electrotypes of rare varieties exhibited in the cases at the British Museum are arranged in chronological order; and such a division of the chief periods of Greek coinage and art may well be followed by the collector, however modest his aims or limited his resources.

The seven periods so defined are as follows:—

1. B.C. 700–480. *Archaic* Art, ending with the Persian Wars.
2. B.C. 480–400. *Transitional and Early Fine Art*, to the end of the Athenian supremacy.
3. B.C. 400–336. *Finest Art.* Age of the Spartan and Theban supremacies.
4. B.C. 336–280. *Later Fine Art.* Age of Alexander and the Diadochi.
5. B.C. 280–190. *Decline of Art.* Age of the Epigoni, etc.
6. B.C. 190–100. *Later Decline of Art.* Age of the Attalids.
7. B.C. 100–1. *Last Stage of Decline of Art.* Age of Mithradates the Great and of Roman dominion.

Fig. 1, Teos, in Ionia ; Fig. 2, Cnidus ; Fig. 3, Lampsacus.

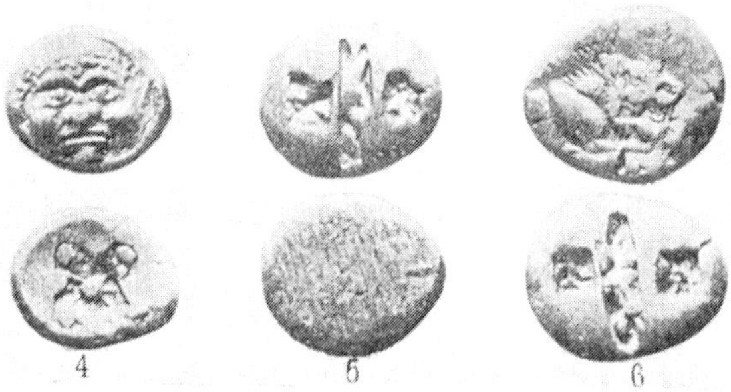

Figs. 4 and 5, Electron coins of Lydia ; Fig. 6, Coin of Miletus.

Fig. 7, Eubœa ; Fig. 8, Athens ; Fig. 9, Thebes.

Each period is again divided geographically in groups, roughly representing: (A) the coins of Asia Minor, Phœnicia, Syria, and Egypt; (B) those of Northern and Central Greece, the Peloponnesus, and the islands of the Ægean; and (C) those of Italy, Sicily, the southern shores of the Mediterranean, and Western Europe.

The three sections in which Greek coins may be defined as relating to their inscriptions are: (A) *Autonomous*, that is those issued by self-governing cities; (B) *Regal* coins bearing the names of kings; and (C) *Imperial*, that is the late coins of Greek cities and islands retaining their right of coinage: on these are the heads of the Roman Emperors, their titles being in Greek.

This classification enables the collector to arrange his coins in trays so that the art of the period under review may be fully realized by reference to several coins of similar types, including those from different places, showing, however, an affinity in character, features, and the artistic rendering of some duplicated subjects. Thus the crude art of the Archaic period is a fitting commencement, gradually leading up to the finest art of the third period in which is included the splendid medallions of Syracuse, which have won so much fame.

The illustrations which are given show some of the most interesting varieties of specimens illustrating the art of the several periods, and represent the early archaic rendering of the die-sinkers, an improvement being seen in the subsequent period, and so on until the climax is reached, and the decline of art set in. They are taken from examples in noted cabinets and in the national collections.

A selection, also illustrated, shows a group of portrait heads of the kings, others typifying the personification of the Greek gods. To become familiar with the portraiture of heathen deities is one of the first steps towards becoming proficient in the study of numismatics. Chief among the gods is Zeus (Jupiter), whose bearded head, crowned with olive or laurel, is familiar to most people. Hades (Pluto), the king of the world of shades, is not unlike Zeus, but he is generally represented as accompanied by Cerberus. Apollo is the personification of youthful beauty, and his full-length figure, unclothed, is seen on many coins of Greece. Hermes (Mercury) is youthful, too, but he wears a close-fitting cap, often with wings attached; as messenger of the gods he carries the winged staff (caduceus). Hephæstus is Vulcan of the Romans, and Herakles the Hercules of the poets, associated in his attributes with the skin of the Numean lion. The bearded head of Pan may be recognized by his pointed ears. Ares (Mars) is not commonly seen on Greek coins. Dionysos (Bacchus) generally holds a wine cup, or is associated with a bunch of grapes—an unmistakable emblem. Helios (Sol), the sun-god, is known by the rays of light around his head. Poseidon (Neptune), with or without his trident, cannot be mistaken. Of goddesses personified there are many. Pallas Athene (Minerva) is one of the most prominent, her helmeted head being familiar to all

Fig. 10, Distater of Thurium ; Fig. 11, Stater of Elis ; Fig. 12, Didrachm of Selinus.

Fig. 13, Tetradrachm of Carthage ; Fig. 14, Tetradrachm of Gela ; Fig. 15, Tetradrachm of Ephesus.

collectors. Hera (Juno) wears a lofty crown, as befits her station among the goddesses. Aphrodite (Venus) the goddess of love, is seldom without Eros (Cupid). Artemis (Diana), as the goddess of nature, carries a bow and a quiver of arrows. Demeter (Ceres) figures on the famous medals of Syracuse; and Isis, the Egyptian goddess, is a noted figure on Greek coins of that country.

The earliest Asiatic Greek coins cover the period B.C. 700–480. Fig. 1 is one from Teos, in Ionia, the emblem, a griffin, being connected with the worship of Dionysos. The Teians afterwards founded Abdera, in Thrace, and the coins struck there have the same emblem. On coins of Cnidus, which was afterwards united with Chersonesus, the lion, the symbol of the sun-god was used. One of these pieces is illustrated in Fig. 2; the head of Aphrodite in an incuse square will be noticed on the reverse. On the obverse of the coin of Lampsacus (Fig. 3) is a Janiform female head, on the reverse the head of Pallas.

Electron was used for the moneys of many of the Asiatic Greek cities; those of Lydia (see Figs. 4 and 5) being the earliest types. Fig. 6 is a coin of Miletus, on the obverse of which is the forepart of a lion.

The types of the coins struck in the cities of Greece during the same period ranging from B.C. 700 to 480 vary somewhat from the Asiatic designs. Fig. 7 is a silver piece of Eubœa; the design on the obverse is intended to represent a wheel of four spokes, on the reverse there is an incuse punch mark.

A Bœotian shield is the emblem on the coin of Thebes shown in Fig. 9, on its reverse a cross within a circle. Fig. 8 represents a very early Athenian coin with the head of Pallas on the obverse. Pallas is also seen on the distater of Thurium, struck about B.C. 390, shown in Fig. 10; the reverse is a bull butting, in the exergue a fish.

Fig. 11 represents a silver stater of Elis, on the obverse is the head of Hera, on the reverse a winged thunderbolt within an olive wreath. On the obverse of Fig. 12, a didrachm of Selinus, the river god Hypsas is seen sacrificing at an altar, in his right hand a patera and in his left a lustral branch.

Many of the coins of Carthage are exceptionally fine, and include rare varieties. Fig. 13 is a tetradrachm of the period B.C. 400–310; on the obverse is the head of Persephone, wearing triple ear-rings, several dolphins in the field; on the reverse the head of a horse and a palm-tree. Another remarkable coin is the one illustrated in Fig. 14; it is a tetradrachm of Gela, in Sicily, on the obverse being an androcephalus bull and on the reverse a biga and Ionic column. A bee was a favourite type in Ephesus; on the reverse of the coin shown in Fig. 15 is also a stag behind a palm-tree.

Reference has been made to the coins of the Greek Kings of Egypt; one of these pieces, struck during the reign of Arsinoe II (B.C. 285–247) is shown in Fig. 16; on its reverse is a cornucopiæ with pendants and grapes. On the very beautiful gold piece of Ptolemy II the conjoined heads of

16 17

GREEK KINGS OF EGYPT.

Fig. 16, Arsinoe II. ; Fig. 17, Ptolemy II.

18 19 18

Fig. 18, Tetradrachm of Syracuse ; Fig. 10, Coin of Tarentum.

20 20

Fig. 20, Obverses of Greek coins, showing (from left to right) heads of Helios, Mercury, and Hermes.

Ptolemy and Arsinoe are seen on the obverse, illustrated in Fig. 17. In Fig. 18 one of the famous tetradrachms of Syracuse is represented. On the obverse is the head of Korê wearing necklace and ear-rings, with dolphins and other attributes; on the reverse Nike crowning the driver of a quadriga with a laurel wreath. One of the finest coins illustrated in this section is the piece of Tarentum, shown in Fig. 19. This city was famous for its gold currency in the middle of the fourth century B.C. In Fig. 20 are the obverses of three coins showing respectively (looking from left to right) the heads of Helios, Mercury, and Hermes. The splendid conception of the old die-sinkers when engraving the figures of the greater deities must have received much of its force from the reality of their belief in them and their power. Note the reverse of Fig. 21, which is a gold stater of Cyrene; on it is Zeus Ammon enthroned, in his right hand an eagle. Fig. 22 is a silver stater of Terina, on the obverse the head of a nymph wearing a sphendome; on the reverse a winged Nike seated on a cippus, in her right hand a caduceus. A silver didrachm of Velia is shown in Fig. 23; on the obverse the head of Pallas wearing a Phrygian helmet, on the reverse a lion.

Apollo is frequently seen on coins of Caulonia, on the reverse of one of these pieces (see Fig. 24), is a stag and the branch of a tree. Fig. 25 represents a stater of Aspendus, on which are two wrestlers on the obverse, and a slinger on the reverse, in the field the triskeles.

Fig. 27 shows the usual types of biga and quadriga. Another illustration of the Greek series is a fine gold stater of Cyrene, on the reverse of which is Zeus Ammon, holding a patera in his right hand and in his left a lotus-headed staff (see Fig. 26).

Fig. 21, Gold Stater of Cyrene ; Fig. 22, Silver Stater of Terina ; Fig. 23, Didrachm of Velia ; Fig. 24, Coin of Caulonia ; Fig. 25, Stater of Aspendus ; Fig. 26, Gold Stater of Cyrene.

Fig. 27, Usual types of biga and quadriga.

IV

COINS OF ANCIENT ROME AND THE REPUBLICAN ERA

CHAPTER IV

COINS OF ANCIENT ROME AND THE REPUBLICAN ERA

The æs and its divisions—Silver and bronze family and consular coins —Gold and silver of the Republic.

THERE is no branch of numismatics which stirs up the imagination of the collector or incites his curiosity so much as the study of the coins of Ancient Rome. It carries him back to times when history and mythology meet; and when deciphering the inscriptions—often abbreviated—he realizes that what we to-day call fables were to the users of those coins very real. The foundations of Rome were laid when pagan worship had scarcely taken shape, and the story of its fabulous origin is read on one of the commonest reverses, that of the suckling of Remus and Romulus, the reputed founders, by a wolf.

The beautiful coinage of Greece was minted long before the Romans struck their famous medallions. But quite early they began to cast their ponderous currency based on the as or æs, originally of twelve ounces. At first the bronze of standard weight was square or oblong, but such pieces when genuine are now rare, and those specimens obtainable are of circular form. Servius Tullius, B.C. 578, promulgated a new constitution, and he classed the citizens according to the wealth they possessed. Their possessions were numbered by the bronze asses they were able to produce from their storehouse: the *æs libra*, or pound of brass, although coined, was taled or weighed when handed over in exchange for goods or cattle. The connection between money and cattle is important to remember in that the Latin *pecunia* is derived from *pecu*, cattle.

The first pieces were uninscribed but designated by the emblems upon them. The ox was probably used first, then followed others. Such pieces, however, may well be remembered among the myths of currency, and passed by as they are now almost unattainable.

It was when the as, or pound of bronze, became circular that it was a true coin. It was the unit of the Roman Mint. The multiples of the as are dupondius (two asses), tripondius (three asses), quadrussis (four asses), and decussis (ten asses). The parts of the as—and in those divisions collectors chiefly become familiar with ancient moneys of Rome—consist of semis (half-as or six unciæ), quincux (five unciæ), triens (third of an as or two unciæ), quadrans (fourth of an as or three unciæ), sextans (sixth of an as or two unciæ), and uncia (twelfth or one ounce). Perhaps the most important thing for a collector to remember when arranging his cabinet or attempting to classify new acquisitions is that almost from the first there was

28

29

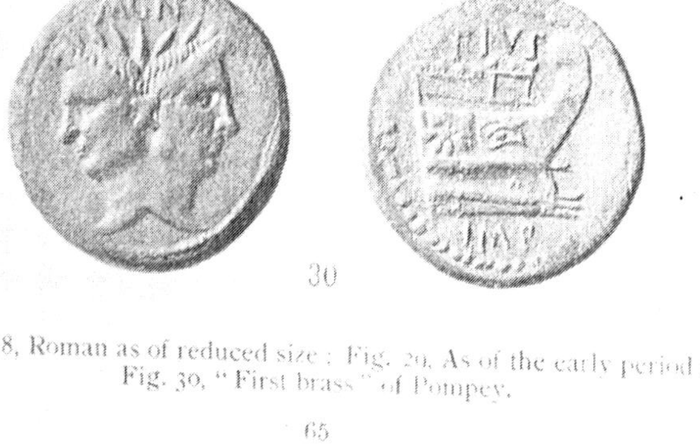

30

Fig. 28, Roman as of reduced size ; Fig. 29, As of the early period ; Fig. 30, " First brass " of Pompey.

a steady downward tendency at the Roman Mint, and from matters of economy or from personal avarice mint-masters reduced the standard weight of the as, and proportionately of its divisions. Thus, later pieces of the bronze currency, although they may represent higher values, are often smaller and lighter. Although there are some exceptions, the distinguishing marks of value come to the aid of the collector, and these, supplemented by the known emblems, used chiefly on certain parts of the as, help to separate the apparent discrepancies. The prevailing emblems are as follows:—

1. The sign of the as, the unit, is **I**, the type of the obverse is the head of the two-faced Janus; that of the reverse the prow of a vessel. On coins of later dates the word "ROMA" frequently appears.

2. The mark of the semis is the letter **S**, both with and without globules. The types vary, sometimes a bull or a wheel, but in the later dates mostly the head of Jupiter, laureated.

3. The mark of the quincux is the letter **V**, and five globules; the type is a cross.

4. The triens is distinguished by four globules; its type is the head of Minerva.

5. The mark of the quadrans is three globules; and its type is the head of Hercules.

6. The sextans is marked by two globules; and its type is the head of Mercury.

7. The uncia is known by one globule, and its type is usually a spear-head or Roma.

The above-mentioned characteristics should be sufficient to enable collectors to determine most of the specimens from the authorized mints of ancient Rome which come into their possession; it may, however, be well to remind the amateur that the as in most of its divisions was minted in other places besides Rome itself, and not always strictly in adherence to the well-defined sizes and weights then prevailing in the city; the types of such pieces vary, too, often being governed by local beliefs. The as is also met with in the cities of Magna Græcia, where Roman bronze coins circulated with late Greek silver.

It is the as of large size that collectors like to secure. Its type, the double-headed Janus, seems familiar, for it is from that pagan deity we still call the first month of the year. In Stevenson's "Dictionary of Roman Coins" we are reminded that Janus was represented with two faces, according to some because of the alliance between the Romans and the Sabines, and by others because of his knowledge of the past as well as of the future. The prow of the ship of the reverse is typical of the vessel which is supposed to have brought Saturn to Italy, and it was in the Temple of Saturn that the Roman treasury was deposited. Fig. 28 shows a small-sized as with the two-faced Janus on the obverse, and the prow of the vessel on the reverse. In Fig. 29 is given the obverse of an as of the early period, the original in the author's collection is a finely patinated specimen. Fig. 30 represents a bronze coin of Pompey, the type of the obverse the Janus head, and that of the reverse the prow of the vessel.

Concurrently with the use of bronze coins, the size of which had been gradually diminishing, there came into existence a new type of coin which was eventually to take the place of the more inconvenient pieces. Three centuries before the Christian era dawned, the third Samnite War was raging. It was then that the innovation crept in. The new coinage of silver began not in the city itself but in Campania, where it was minted for the payment of the troops. The earlier pieces were didrachms, and bore the head of Hercules on the obverse, on the reverse being the famous representation of Remus and Romulus already alluded to; under this group was inscribed the place-name "ROMANO." There are others of that period with the helmeted head of Mars on the obverse, a horse's head and ears of corn on the reverse. At that time the coins bore the inscription "ROMANO" on a panel.

A little later the name became "ROMA," and it was in relief, not incuse as it had been in the earlier varieties. Another change came half a century later, when the Romans had adopted Pallas as the type of their city personified. On the obverses the goddess's head is helmeted, on the reverses the Dioscuri gallop to right (see Fig. 31): these pieces are the early denarii, the size and type of which was mainly preserved throughout the Consular coinage. Castor and Pollux, the twin brethren, were the gods of sailors, merchants, and travellers, and it is said were accepted with satisfaction by every class as the type of silver currency.

From the year B.C. 217 until the Imperial issues the coins of Rome are classed as Family coins. Those having the right to issue them were the officers of the Republic and the generals commanding the armies.

The Family series are by no means difficult to collect, and may be secured in fine preservation for from two to three shillings each, although there are rarities, and some of exceptional value. In issues of the period dating onward until the close of the Republican era there was some use of bronze or copper, but they were mainly of silver. The quadriga became the favourite type, and the value mark "X" was mostly used. In Fig. 32 is shown a denarius of Sulla, one of the Cornelia family; on the reverse a military figure stands in a triumphal quadriga, crowned by a Victory flying overhead; in the exergue L[ucius] SULLA.

Towards the year B.C. 104 the name "ROMA" was omitted. In that year "ROMA" rarely appears, and her place was taken by a multiplicity of deities, Apollo, Saturn, Hercules, and Vulcan being the most frequently seen. From this time to the beginning of the Imperial period a greater irregularity of type and size is noticeable. The issuers were chiefly denoted by their family names in full, prefixed by the distinguishing initials of their first names. The types vary much, for many of the emblems refer to events in their lives or in the past of their families.

In the early days the minting of money was frequently shown accompanied by minting instruments, such, for instance, the coins of the Carisia gens, on

ROMAN COINS OF THE CONSULAR PERIOD.

Fig. 31, Early type ; Fig. 32, Denarius of Sulla (Cornelia gens) ; Fig. 33, Julia gens ; Fig. 34, Mark Antony ; Fig. 35, Octavius ; Fig. 36, Julia gens.

IMPERIAL SERIES.

Fig. 37, Julius Cæsar ; Fig. 38, Augustus ; Fig. 39, Tiberius ; Fig. 40, Caligula ; Fig. 41, Claudius ; Fig. 42, Nero.

which is the inscription "CVR.X.FL.S.C." and the legend "MONETA." The old dies were struck by hand and were soon broken; hence it is that there are so many minor variations in dies purporting to represent the same device. As we have seen, the coins of the Republic generally bore the head of some deity, for it was not until the Senate placed the head of Julius Cæsar upon the pieces struck in his honour that any personal portraits were attempted by the die-sinkers. There is an extensive and very interesting series of coins of the Julia family. The best known is the one with the type of the elephant crushing the serpent. An interesting variety is shown in Fig. 33; on the obverse is a female head, and on the reverse the inscription "CAESAR" and a military trophy. During the last portion of the Republican era there were coins bearing the head of Julius struck by the magistrates and generals by order of the Senate, others which had upon them the names of Lepidus, Antony, and Octavius. That shown in Fig. 34 bears the head of Mark Antony on the obverse, and that of M. Lepidus on the reverse. The beautiful coin of Octavius, illustrated in Fig. 35, is in the British Museum. The one shown in Fig. 36 is also in the National Collection; it was illustrated and described by Stevenson in his "Dictionary of Roman Coins," as a silver piece of the Julia family; on the obverse is the head of Brutus, and on the reverse the *pileus*, or Cap of Liberty, between two daggers. That brings the series to a fitting conclusion in that it was Octavius who afterwards took the name of Augustus, and assuming the Imperial purple heralded in the era of Rome under its Emperors.

As a convenience for those about to form a cabinet of Republican denarii, the following table, giving both surnames and family names of most of the issues procurable, should be helpful:—

SURNAME.	FAMILY.	SURNAME.	FAMILY.
Acisculus	Valeria.	Catullus	Valeria.
Agrippa	Luria.	Celer	Cassia.
,,	Vipsania.	Celsus	Papia.
Ahala	Servilia.	Censorinus	Marcia.
Ahenobarbus	Domitia.	Cerco	Lutatia.
Albinus	Postumia.	Cestianus	Plætoria.
Antiaticus	Mænia.	Cethegus	Cornelia.
Aquinus	Cæcilia.	Chilo, Cilo	Flaminia.
Asiagenes	Cornelia.	Cinna	Cornelia.
Atratinus	Sempronia.	Cocles	Horatia.
Augurinus	Minucia.	Cordus	Mucia.
Bala	Ælia.	Cossus	Cornelia.
Balbus	Acilia.	Costa	Pedania.
,,	Antonia.	Cotta	Aurelia.
,,	Atia.	Crassipes	Furia.
,,	Cornelia.	Crassus	Licinia.
,,	Nævia.	,,	Canidia.
,,	Thoria.	Crispinus	Quinctia.
Bassus	Betiliena.	Croto	Metilia.
Bibulus	Calpurnia.	Dossenus	Rubria.
Blandus	Rubellia.	Fabatus	Roscia.
Blasio	Cornelia.	Faustus	Cornelia.
Brocchus	Furia.	Felix	Cornelia.
Brutus	Junia.	Flaccus	Rutilia.
Buca	Æmilia.	,,	Valeria.
Bursio	Julia.	Flavius	Decimia.
Cæicianus	Cassia.	Florus	Aquillia.
Cæpio	Servilia.	Fostulus	Pompeia.
Cæsar	Julia.	Frugi	Calpurnia.
Caldus	Cœlia.	Gal[eria]	Memmia.
Capella	Nævia.	Galba	Sulpicia.
Capito	Fonteia.	Gallus	Asinia.
,,	Maria.	,,	Caninia.
,,	Oppia.	Geminus	Aburia.
Capitolinus	Petillia.	Geta	Hosidia.
Carbo	Papiria.	Grag[ulus]	Antestia.
Casca	Servilia.	Gracchus	Sempronia.
Cato	Porcia.	Hemic...*	Flavia.

SURNAME.	FAMILY.
Hypsæus	Plautia.
Judex	Vettia.
Junianus	Licinia.
Kalenus	Fufia.
Labeo	Fabia.
Labienus	Atia ?
Læca	Porcia.
Lamia	Ælia.
Lariscolus	Accoleia.
Lentulus	Cornelia.
Lepidus	Æmilia.
Libo	Marcia.
,,	Scribonia.
Licinus	Porcia.
Limetanus	Mamilia.
Longinus	Cassia.
Longus	Mussidia.
Lucanus	Terentia.
Lupercus	Gallia.
Macer	Licinia.
,,	Sepullia.
Magnus	Pompeia.
Malleolus	Poblicia.
Marcellinus	Cornelia.
Marcellus	Claudia.
Maridainus	Cossutia.
Maximus	Egnatia.
,,	Fabia.
Mensor	Farsuleia.
Messalia	Valeria.
Metullus	Cæcilia
Molo	Pomponia.
Murcus	Statia.
Murena	Licinia.
Mus	Decia.
Musa	Pomponia.
Naso	Axia.
Natta	Pinaria.
Nerva	Cocceia.
,,	Licinia.
,,	Silia.
Nomentanus	Atilia.
Nonianus	Considia.
Otho	Salvia.
Pætus	Ælia.
,,	Considia.
Palikanus	Lollia.
Pansa	Vibia.
Paullus	Æmilia.
Philippus	Marcia.

SURNAME.	FAMILY.
Philus	Furia.
Pictor	Fabia.
Piso	Calpurnia.
Pitio	Sempronia.
Pius	Cæcilia.
,,	Pompeia.
Plancus	Munatia.
,,	Plautia.
Platorinus	Sulpicia.
Pulcher	Claudia.
Purpureo	Fabia.
Quinctilianus	Nonia.
Reginus	Antistia.
Regulus	Livineia.
Restio	Antia.
Rocus	Creperia.
Rufus	Aurelia.
,,	Cordia.
,,	Lucilia.
,,	Mescinia.
,,	Minucia.
,,	Plotia.
,,	Pompeia.
,,	Pomponia.
,,	Sulpicia.
Rullus	Servilia.
Sabinus	Minatia.
,,	Tituria.
,,	Vettia.
Sabula	Cossutia.
Salinator	Oppia.
Saranus	Atilia.
Saserna	Hostilia.
Saturninus	Appuleia.
Saxula	Clovia.
Scæva	Junia.
Scarpus	Pinaria.
Scaurus	Æmilia.
,,	Aurelia.
Scipio	Cornelia.
Secundus	Arria.
Ser . . . •	Manlia.
Silanus	Junia.
Silianus	Licinia.
Silus	Sergia.
Sisenna	Cornelia.
Spinther	Cornelia.
Stolo	Licinia.
Strabo	Volteia.
Sufenas	Nonia.

SURNAME.	FAMILY.	SURNAME.	FAMILY.
Sulla	Cornelia.	Tubulus	Hostilia.
Sulpicianus	Quinctia.	Tullus	Mæcilia.
Surdinus	Nævia.	Turdus	Papiria.
Talna	Juventia.	Turpilianus	Petronia.
Tampilus	Bæbia.	Unimanus	Claudia.
Taurus	Statilia.	Vaala	Numonia
Thermus	Minucia.	Varro	Terentia.
Torquatus	Manlia.	Varus	Vibia.
Trigeminus	Curiatia.	Vetus	Antistia.
Trio	Lucretia.	Vitulus	Voconia.
Trogus	Maria.	Volusus	Valeria.

The terminals of the names inscribed on these coins have not been satisfactorily determined.

IMPERIAL SILVER AND GOLD.

Fig. 43, Galba ; Fig. 44, Otho ; Fig. 45, Vitellius ; Fig. 46, Vespasian ; Fig. 47, Titus ; Fig. 48, Domitian.

SILVER DENARII.

Fig. 49, Nerva ; Fig. 50, Commodus ; Fig. 51, Antoninus Pius ; Fig. 52, Faustina, the Elder ; Fig. 53, Lucilla ; Fig. 54, Aurelian.

V

THE COINS OF THE TWELVE GREAT CÆSARS

Fig. 55, Sestertius of Julius Cæsar (Posthumous).

Fig. 56, Augustus (Restoration coin).

Fig. 57, Augustus (Restored by Tiberius).

CHAPTER V

THE COINS OF THE TWELVE GREAT CÆSARS

The Roman Mint—Coins and medallions of historic interest—The gods of the heathen—Triumphs, emblems, and inscriptions.

IT seems fitting that the coins of the twelve Great Cæsars should be reviewed apart from those—many debased in quality of metal and in size—of the Emperors and usurpers who followed them. Yet the earlier reigns do not by any means contain all that is beautiful or rare in the Imperial series! They do, however, lend tone and impart dignity to the cabinet in which they form a fitting place of prominence. Of different sizes to many of the later coins, they may, with advantage, be classed by themselves. The most frequently met with are, of course, the splendid series of sestertii, or first brass, but they are supplemented by larger pieces known as medallions, mostly commemorative, and probably issued as medals and retained as such. The so-called large brass coins were minted from an amalgam of tin and copper, and the dies were carefully prepared and the coins well struck. With equal precision the dupondii, or second brass, were minted, and many of the dies for the smaller pieces being in no way inferior to the larger coins and medallions. The small coins or third brass of the early Emperors were unimportant and need not be taken much note of.

The gold, silver, and brass of the early Cæsars offer many attractions to the collector, especially to the student of history—the history of a country which attained an exceptional status in the world. When the Imperial purple was assumed by Augustus a new departure was made, and although many of the offices which had been filled by men associated with the minting of money were retained, they were to some extent sinecures. The Emperors of Rome acquired the sole right to coin gold aureii and silver denarii, the mintage of brass resting with the Senate. The letters S.C. (*Senatus consulto*) are conspicuous on many of the fine bronze and brass pieces, denoting by whose authority they were issued.

The story of the mint is full of interest. That of the Roman Mint especially so, for it reveals the vast resources of that great Empire, and of its mineral wealth mined in countries far removed from the Imperial City. Mention of the mines reminds us of the hardships of those who dug for gold, silver, and copper, with which to fill the treasure-house of their masters. In these mines many Christian slaves worked; some, too, may have taken part in the actual minting of money. Mints were multiplied in later years, and after the division of the Empire by Diocletian they were set up in many of the conquered countries which became Roman provinces.

The coins and medals of the earlier reigns—

Fig. 58, First brass of Tiberius.

Fig. 59, First brass of Claudius.

Fig. 60, First brass of Claudius.

especially of the twelve Great Cæsars—were very beautiful. The portraiture and inscriptions stood out in bold relief. On the obverses the heads of the Emperors and those of their Empresses were excellent likenesses. So true to life were they that it is said the family traits can be seen on coins which have hitherto been unknown, thus assisting the expert in naming them. It is a fact that most of the ordinary issues, however rubbed the inscriptions are, can be named from the mere outline of the profile of the head on the obverses.

It is natural, perhaps, that the deities who were supposed to govern the lives of the people and to give successes to the army should figure on the coins. Indeed, the reverses in all the metals are usually occupied with the representation of deities or their emblems. The Romans thought it wise to propitiate them all. Their gods of renown figured with almost equal frequency; thus in a single tray of coins may be inspected the Roman idea of the personification of Juno, Minerva, Vesta, Ceres, Diana, Mars, Mercury, Neptune, Jupiter, Vulcan, and Apollo.

It is said that the figure of Jupiter on the coins was copied from the famous statues of Phidias and Lysippus, and every detail of form and of his attributes were carefully executed. Many old customs and heathen rites may be traced in the attributes of Juno, the queen of the goddesses. Minerva, the Greek Athene, is seen on many fine medallions of the early Cæsars, and it was that goddess whose head was chosen to personify the City of Rome on the coins of the Republic. The huntress

Diana is seen on both Consular and Imperial coins, especially is she pictured on the later issues of Gallienus. Vulcan is a familiar figure, and is at once recognized by his anvil and hammer by all who know him to be the god of workers in metal and of artisans. There were plenty of statues of Venus from which the die-sinkers of the Roman mint-masters could model their effigies of that goddess; and the legend "VENVS GENETRIX" is seen on coins of most of the Empresses, especially on those of Faustina the Elder, and Lucilla. The sacred fire of Vesta is depicted on her altars, and the goddess is recognized by her attributes.

Mars, originally the god of the agriculturist, became the god of war. The tillers of the soil were enrolled as soldiers in time of need, and welcomed Mars as their preserver at all times. The numerous inscriptions in honour of the god may be exemplified in the one which reads "MARTI CONSERVATORI AVG N" [*ostri*], (*To Mars the Preserver of our Emperor*). The inscription "HERCVLES VICTORI" is often met with, for Hercules was a favourite protector. The early beliefs of the Romans were strong, and for the most part they were clung to tenaciously. The emblems on the coins they used had a real meaning to them; thus Apollo was to them a preserver much sought after in times of plague and disease. In the reign of Gallienus, the god is represented by a centaur, Apollo having been taught the art of healing by the Centaur Chiron—so the legend ran. Apollo was the most frequently used type on the earlier coins of Constantine. Then came the Emperor's conversion

61

Fig 61, First brass of Nero.

62

Fig. 62, First brass of Nero.

63

Fig. 63, First brass of Galba.

to Christianity, and suddenly the heathen gods which had been such a stumbling-block to the early Christian Church were banished from the Roman coins—they disappeared before the mystic symbol of the Cross, which was henceforth to take their place.

Just as the religions of Rome are made clear by the inscriptions on "a few old coins," so the daily life of its citizens may be better understood by their study. The games in which the people revelled are pictured. Those cruel sports were, it is said, first instituted to appease the heathen gods in time of pestilence. They are shown on coins of Augustus who held their sixth celebration; and they are again pictured on coins of Domitian and Septimus Severus, as well as on some of the later pieces. On a coin of Domitian the procession of boys and girls mentioned by Horace is depicted; and on another coin some of the animals killed in the so-called games are represented. The hopes and aspirations of men were personified, and used as emblems on many of the coins. Thus special prominence is given to Peace, Plenty, Concord, Eternity, Providence, Faith, Joy, and Equity.

The common objects of interest around them gave the die-sinkers plenty of scope for their skill, for the works of man, too, were conspicuous, especially the peaceful arts. Very valuable are the coins on which these were depicted to students of Roman history; for on them are seen faithfully and accurately represented architectural buildings and sculpture, much of which has perished, and that which remains to the present day is disfigured or has lost its original beauty.

There are basilicas, bridges, aqueducts, columns, tombs, arches, and temples. In the last-named group are temples which had been erected to Jupiter, Janus, Venus, Mars, and Concord. The fine arch erected in honour of Nero on the Capitoline Hill is seen on a first brass of that wicked ruler. Such arches are conspicuous on coins of Domitian and Trajan, whose Column is immediately recognized. A splendid representation of the Flavian Amphitheatre (the Colosseum) is on a first brass of Titus. In a city so full of exquisite marbles as Rome was in the days of its greatness, it is no wonder that some of the works of art, so few of which remain now, were chosen as the types for the reverses of the large brass or sestertii of the twelve Great Cæsars.

The inscriptions on Roman coins are a fruitful source of information. It is true they are much abbreviated, but that does not deter the enthusiastic numismatist from deciphering them. The army of Rome maintained the greatness of the Empire, hence it is that allusions to the Imperial troops are so frequently met with. It is quite easy to recognize the legends referring to them, for the word *exercitas* (army) is often mentioned. The most complete set of allusions is found on the coins and medals of Hadrian, on which are recorded the doings of the eleven armies of Britannia, Cappadocia, Dacia, Hispania, Judæa, Germania, Mauretania, Norica, Parthia, Rhætia, and Syria. In explanation of these legends it may be pointed out that the concord of the army was of paramount importance, hence the frequent legend, "CONCORDIA EXERCITVVM": the loyalty of

64

Fig. 64, First brass of Vitellius.

65

Fig. 65, First brass of Vespasian.

66

Fig. 66, First brass of Titus.

the army was of equal value, thus we find on the reverses of many "FIDES EXERCITVVM"; the glory and virtue of the soldiers is in like manner commemorated. The Roman legions were early mentioned; thus on silver denarii of Mark Antony, Severus, Carausius, and others, they are referred to, and typified by their standards. On the later coins of Constantine the Great the eagles of Rome were displaced for the labarum, on which was the monogram of Christ.

It is impossible here to do more than mention a few of the chief inscriptions which record special purposes of mintage or give some new glory to the Emperor in whose honour they were struck, and whose effigy they bore. The consulate so often inscribed was a relic of the Consular period, when two men of renown were appointed to rule for the year. During Imperial power the Emperors frequently nominated themselves or their sons. The change had come when Julius was appointed Dictator. It was the surname of the Julia family which was selected as the title for the coming wearer of the purple, and too frequently a Cæsar was proclaimed by the soldiers in a moment of victory without any thought of the capacity of that soldier prince to rule over the destinies of the Empire of Rome.

The superscription of the Emperors brings to mind vividly scenes in Biblical history. "Whose is the image and superscription?" was the question asked by our Lord. And we find the answer before us, as it was in days gone by, when we inspect a denarius of Tiberius. For there it is written. In clear lettering we realize that the Emperor Tiberius ascribed to himself equality with the Divine. He was the high priest of the heathen—their "PONTIFEX MAXIMVS."

The empty honour of being Father of his Country was given to Augustus, and is seen on his coins on which is read "PATER PATRIÆ." Deceased emperors were often accorded deification, thus consecration coins struck after death were inscribed "DIVVS," and those in memory of their wives "DIVA."

The coinage of the twelve Great Cæsars, as we have seen, presents an historical series of coins minted in gold aureii (AV), silver denarii (AR), and brass sestertii and dupondii (Æ). In addition to the pieces bearing the Imperial portraits there are those coins struck by and in honour of others connected with the Emperors; those collectable under those respective reigns may be gathered from the following table :—

Augustus, Emperor	B.C. 27–A.D. 14
Julia, wife of Augustus	
Agrippa	
Tiberius, Emperor	A.D. 14–37
Caius	
Caius and Lucius	
Drusus, Senior	
Antonia	
Drusus, Junior	
Germanicus	
Agrippina, wife of Germanicus	
Caligula	A.D. 37–41
Claudius	A.D. 41–54
Agrippina, wife of Claudius	
Nero	A.D. 54–68

67

Fig. 67, First brass of Domitian.

68

Fig. 68, First brass of Nerva.

69

Fig. 69, First brass of Trajan.

Galba	A.D. 68–69
Otho	A.D. 69
Vitellius	A.D. 69
Vespasian	A.D. 69–79
Domitilla, wife of Vespasian	
Titus	A.D. 79–81
Julia, daughter of Titus	
Domitian	A.D. 81–96
Domitia, wife of Domitian	

When the coins of this period are compared with authentic busts of the Emperors and Empresses in the galleries of the British Museum, the skill of the Roman die-sinkers is admired, and their faithful portraiture recognized. The illustrations given in this chapter are all either gold aureïi or silver denarii. Fig. 37 represents a coin of Julius Cæsar struck after he had been made Dictator, the inscription of the obverse reading "CAESAR . DIC"; on the reverse is the legend "L . BVCA," and a winged caduceus laid across a Consular fasces, an axe, a globe, and two hands clasped. Fig. 38 is a fine coin of Augustus, on the reverse the inscription "C . CAES." and in the exergue, "AVGVS . F[illius]." relating to his adoption by Julius.

The so-called "Tribute penny" of Tiberius, by no means a scarce piece, is shown in Fig. 39. A denarius of Caius Cæsar (Caligula) is shown in Fig. 40, the inscription on the reverse is one frequently seen on Roman coins; it is "S . P . Q . R.," signifying *Senatus Populusque Romanus* (The Senate and the Roman People). The illustration, Fig. 41, is taken from a rare coin of Claudius in the British Museum. It is especially interesting because of the triumphal arch on the reverse, inscribed "DE BRITANN," commemorating the conquest of Britain. Fig. 42 represents an exceedingly fine gold aureus of Nero. On the reverse Nero is represented standing, his head radiated. In his left hand he holds a Victory, and in his right a laurel branch.

Most of the coins of Galba, a denarius of whose reign is illustrated in Fig. 43, are scarce. Well-preserved coins of the short reign of Otho are exceedingly difficult to obtain; the one shown in Fig. 44 is a very fine specimen in the British Museum. Concord is seen on the reverse of the coin of Vitellius, in Fig. 45. Vespasian used a variety of reverses, that illustrated in Fig. 46 showing a bull, was issued during the sixth consulate of the Emperor. The coins of Titus in all the metals are remarkable for the fine series commemorative of the capture of Judæa, the one illustrated in Fig. 47 showing a weeping maiden beneath a palm-tree. Domitian, the last of the twelve Great Cæsars, issued many fine silver pieces, some with scarce reverses. The one illustrated in Fig. 48 represents the legendary story of the wolf and the twins, in the exergue a small boat.

The foregoing illustrations represent the series issued by the Emperors in silver and gold. Concurrent with these the Senate struck many beautiful sestertii, and some of the larger medallions, as well as dupondii. The collector can gather many of these, but in fine preservation some of them are

Fig. 70, First brass of Hadrian.

Fig. 71, First brass of Antoninus Pius.

Fig. 72, First brass of Antoninus Pius.

extremely rare; the inexperienced must beware of forgeries, of which there are many.

The reign of Augustus was prolific in contributing to the series of bronze, especially in the early commemorative pieces, the one illustrated in Fig. 55 being an example of the coins struck in honour of Julius Cæsar (after his death); on the obverse is the deified head of Julius, around it the inscription "DIVOS IVLIVS," on the reverse the head of Octavius (Augustus), and the legend "CAESAR . DIVI . F." Fig. 56 is a large brass struck as a restoration coin in honour of Augustus, around whose laureated head on the obverse is the legend, "DIVVS AVGVSTVS," by Nerva, whose inscription can be read around "S C" on the reverse. Another restitution coin is shown in Fig. 57, on the reverse of which Augustus is represented seated before an altar. On the reverse is the name of Tiberius, in whose reign it was struck. A first brass of Tiberius, illustrated in Fig 58, shows an altar with a figure of Victory on either side. In the exergue is the legend "ROM ET AVG." According to Stevenson this coin was struck at Lyons, where a temple and an altar had been erected by the Gauls "to Rome and Augustus." On a fine piece of Claudius illustrated in Fig. 59, Hope holds a flower in her right hand. On another coin of Claudius, shown in Fig. 60, there is a triumphal arch surmounted by an equestrian statue.

There are quite a number of fine reverses of Nero; the one shown in Fig. 61 is that of Roma seated, holding a figure of Victory in her hand, in the field the letters "S.C." Another coin of the same Emperor shown in Fig. 62 represents Nero riding on horseback, followed by a horseman carrying a vexilium.

Many of the first brass of Galba are rare, one exceptionally fine piece, illustrated in Fig. 63, bears the inscription "S P Q R OB CIV. SER." On the reverse of a first brass of Vitellius (Fig. 64) Mars is seen carrying a trophy and a spear, the legend round it reading "MARS VICTOR."

A fine first brass of Vespasian commemorating the victories of the Emperor's armies in Judæa is given in Fig. 65; on that of Titus, in Fig. 66, Peace holds an olive branch commemorating the peace then concluded. The last illustration of the coins of the Great Cæsars is a first brass of Domitian, see Fig. 67; on the reverse the Emperor is represented clasping hands with a youth in a toga in front of an altar, near by being a soldier, and a standard-bearer. In concluding this chapter, the attention of the reader is drawn to Fig. 73, a coin struck in honour of the Empress Livia, the fourth wife of Augustus, on which is the legend "IVSTITIA," and to Fig. 74, a large memorial brass of Agrippina, on the reverse of which is a carpentium drawn by two mules.

Fig. 73, Coin of the Empress Livia ; Fig. 74, Memorial coin of the Empress Agrippina.

Fig. 75, Sabina (wife of Hadrian) ; Fig. 76, First brass of Faustina (daughter of Antoninus Pius).

VI

ROMAN CURRENCY UNDER THE LATER EMPERORS

CHAPTER VI

ROMAN CURRENCY UNDER THE LATER EMPERORS

Empire-builders and the inscriptions on their coins—Debasing the currency—Late Byzantine coins.

AFTER the division of the Empire under Domitian, the Emperors who immediately succeeded him appear to have specially favoured the issue of medallions to commemorate the chief events which were then occurring throughout the vast Empire, to which the army was adding every year. They also took every opportunity of altering the dies of the large brass sestertii, and added to their own titles or made mention of the activity going on in the State in each fresh issue. As during the reigns of the earlier Cæsars the coins of later types kept in memory green the ancient faiths, and the deities supposed to preside over the destinies of men and their special occupations; but the coinage was chiefly made use of as a means of recording victories and telling the people in picture form of the triumphs they were achieving and of the buildings being erected to Rome. There seems to have been an educative intent in the numerous medals, clearly read by those who could follow the signs and emblems introduced. In Fig. 67 is given a beautiful coin struck during the twelfth consulate of Domitian; on the reverse the Emperor is seen clasping the hand of a youth in a toga, standing in front of an altar, in proximity being a soldier and a standard-bearer. It is one of many, and as an encouragement to collectors we may repeat the words of Captain Smith, an old authority on Roman coins: "The medals of this Emperor are abundant and cheap."

The emblems on the coins of Nerva are also very instructive, and elucidative of the history of the times; one of the commoner types is two hands, joined, emblematical of good faith, others of a like character are numerous. On some there is a military trophy affixed to the prow of a vessel, symbolical that the army and the navy concurred in the election of Nerva, who as Emperor in his short reign of two years accomplished much. On the obverse of the first brass represented in Fig. 68 is the legend "VEHICVLATIONE ITALIAE REMMISSA." This, another remarkably interesting piece, on which is seen two mules feeding, liberated from their yokes, commemorates Nerva giving relief to the people of Italy from the oppression under which they had suffered—an event which took place in A.D. 97. Towards the last part of the reign of the Emperor he was assisted by Trajan who succeeded him, and afterwards struck pieces recording the deification of his predecessor; these may be distinguished by the inscription "DIVVS NERVA."

For twenty years Trajan ruled. He was an empire-

Fig. 77, First brass of Lucius Verus.

Fig. 78, First brass of Commodus,

Fig. 79. First brass of Crispina.

builder of no mean order, and he caused some of the finest buildings Roman architects can boast of to be put up. Among those commemorated on his coins is the stone bridge across the Danube, and, of course, his masterpiece, the great Column in the Forum. That shown in Fig. 69 bears the legend "OPTIMO PRINCIPI," indicating the title of *Optimus Princeps* which had been conferred on Trajan by the Senate. The coins of Trajan relating to Britain are of special interest to British collectors; on the reverse of one Britannia is seated, a spear in her hand, her foot upon a rock, a spiked shield or buckler at her side; in the exergue the inscription "BRITANNIA." It was from commemorative pieces such as that, telling of the victories in Britain, that we derive the emblem so familiar still on our own bronze coinage. To the old Roman it told of a conquered nation subdued, another colony planted; to the Britisher of to-day the emblem calls to mind the familiar stirring song telling that "Britannia rules the waves," and that her sons will never bow in slavery to another conqueror!

Hadrian was in Antioch when Trajan died, in A.D. 118. He was then declared Emperor, and continued to lead the armies, with whose aid he had already won many triumphs. He is remembered as one of those Roman generals who marched with his legions through Britain and left his mark in the building of the famous wall, fragments of which may still be seen, and which are treasured as the chief antiquarian records of the presence of the Romans in this country. The names and titles on the coins of Hadrian are a little puzzling; as an instance, the one referring to his adoption by Trajan and to his being the grandson of Nerva, which reads: "IMP. CAES. HADRIANVS. DIVI. NER. TRAI. OPT. FIL." A first brass of Hadrian, showing Ceres holding two wheat-ears and a torch, struck during the third consulate of the Emperor, is given in Fig. 70. Perhaps one of the most remarkable medals of Hadrian is that representing the Emperor destroying by fire the bonds, when he paid out of his own purse the debts of the State, 9,000,000 sestertii—an example to modern statesmen of great wealth!

The medals of Sabina, the wife of Hadrian, confirm the testimony of historians who tell of the beauty of this princess: on the obverses of some of these pieces her hair is arranged terminating with a long braid; on others the hair is bound up tightly at the back of the head. The reverse of the first brass shown in Fig. 75 has for its type Vesta, seated, holding a palladium and sceptre. On a remarkably fine deification medal Sabina is represented as borne on the wings of an eagle to heaven.

Antoninus Pius assumed many names and used them freely on his coins, making his inscriptions no easy matter to define. He had been a successful consul, and had taken a prominent place in the affairs of State during the reign of Hadrian, and his coins tell of the position he held as Emperor in the opinion of the Senate. Fig. 71 is a first brass of his, on the reverse being a decastyle temple on the pediment of which is a figure seated between two

80

81

Figs. 80 and 81, Septimus Severus.

82

83

Figs. 82 and 83, Caracalla.

other figures kneeling. On the reverse of another coin, shown in Fig. 72, Peace is seen in the act of setting fire to a pile of arms with her torch. Fig. 76 is a first brass of Faustina, the daughter of Antoninus Pius, on the reverse of which Lætitia is seen standing. For an example of a silver denarius of Antoninus Pius see Fig. 51, a coin of the Empress Faustinia the Elder, his wife, being given in Fig. 52.

The coins of Commodus are varied in their types. Fig. 50 is a silver denarius of that Emperor, and Fig. 78 a brass coin of special interest, the Emperor being shown sacrificing at a tripod, an attendant in the act of killing a bull, the ceremony being attended by musicians. In Fig. 79 is given a first brass of Crispina, the wife of Commodus; on the reverse Joy holds a wreath and supports a rudder upon a globe.

Septimus Severus became sole Emperor in A.D. 197. He founded many colonies, and was particularly active in Britain, dying at Eboracum (York) A.D. 211. His medallions are good, but most of the silver and brass of ordinary types was poor. It was at that time that the deterioration of the quality of metal began. The specimens of this reign illustrated are exceptionally fine, however; the first, Fig. 80, relates to the victories in Britain, the legend reading "VICTORIAE BRITANNICAE"; and the second, Fig. 81, to the establishment of peace in the Empire after the overthrow of Pescennius Niger. The coins of Julia Domna, the second wife of Severus, are also plentiful.

At this period in Roman history the coins of the

Emperors and their generals are stamped with the lowering of the standard of quality in *every* way. The Emperors themselves were men who showed low and depraved characters, and their medals seem to breathe of murder, rapine, and crime. The chief coins were the impoverished second and third brass and denarii, the quality of which scarcely warrants its being classed as silver, for most of the specimens are only copper washed with silver or tin. Such is the aspect of the trays which contain the coins of Caracalla, Geta, Macrinus, Elagabalus, Alexander, Maximinus, Gordianus I, Balbinus, Pupienus (the coins of this prince are of great rarity), Philippus, Trajanus Decius, Trebonianus Gallus, and others of that age.

Scarcely greater interest centres in the coins of Valerianus, which are for the most part billon and copper. Those in honour of Mariniana, his wife, struck after her death, however, are pleasing, the type of the reverse being the sacred peacock of Juno, around which is read the legend "CONSECRATIO."

The illustrations relating to this period show the decline of art and general deterioration of design. Two scarce coins of Caracalla are shown in Figs. 82 and 83, the reverse of the former representing Security, and the latter Britannia with her hands tied behind her. In Fig. 84, a coin of Geta, Caracalla and Geta, are shown in the act of sacrificing; on another piece of the same prince, Fig. 85, there is a Victory seated on the reverse. Fig. 86 is a fine specimen of the scarce coins of Macrinus. Fig. 87 represents a coin of Elagabalus, who was born at

84

85

Figs. 84 and 85, Geta.

86

87

Fig. 86, Macrinus ; Fig. 87, Elagabalus.

Emesa, where Heliogabalus, from whom he derived his name, was chiefly worshipped ; hence the figure of Sol as the principal emblem on the reverse.

A very interesting group of coins of the later Empresses is given in Figs. 88–91. One of Julia Mæsa, on the reverse of which is Felicity, is shown in Fig. 88 ; and one of Julia Mamæa, having Vesta for its type, in Fig. 89. Gordianus Pius, with Lætitia on the reverse, is represented by Fig. 90 ; and Octacilla Severa in Fig. 91.

Gallienus seems to have issued a vast number of small brass coins, and to have used every ingenuity in varying their reverses. Of the coins of the Emperors which followed little need be said. It was Diocletian who put the currency on a somewhat better footing and introduced a new coin, which he named a follis, about the size of the English half-penny, of bronze.

The finds of Roman coins in this and other countries have brought to light many varieties, so much so that it is possible to collect hundreds all different, and yet having a similarity in the profile portraiture of the Emperor. Such coins are interesting to the collector, but not to the art connoisseur. It is worth noting that while many of the discoveries of coins show that they had been buried in a camp or on the site of a mint, quite a number of them have been found near some ancient well ; the Romans held their wells to be sacred, and believed such a place to be the safest, for none would rob a sacred spot for fear of the gods. Fortunately, those hoards have been veritable hunting-grounds for the present-day collector, who sorts them out and finds delight even in those almost undecipherable—if it gives him a new reverse.

The coins of the Lower Empire are indeed so numerous, and their issuers came and went with such rapidity, that the collector is lost in the maze of the multiplicity of monarchs and in the variety of their small brass. These little coins, presenting so many interesting reverses, are either billon or copper, sometimes washed with silver. Some of the dies were crude in their designs, although most of them are emblematical of the later Roman deities, varied after the adoption of the Christian faith by Constantine by emblems of the new religion; dropped in the days of Julian the Apostate, who revived the rites of the heathen gods, and restored them to the place of honour on the coinage.

The rarity of these little pieces vary; they may, however, be roughly classified under three divisions, denoting their approximate relative values. The common coins are those of Valerian, Gallien, Salonica, Postumus, Claudius Gothicus, Victorian, Tetricus, Aurelian, Tacitus, Probus, Diocletian, Maximian, Constantius I, Crispus, Constantine II, Constans, Licinius, and a few others. Among the scarcer varieties may be mentioned Salonin, Quintillus, Severina, Carus, Carinus, Numerian, Carausius, Allectus, Fausta, Julian II, and Honorius. There are a few rare reigns which are difficult to obtain in fine preservation. Among them are those of Lælian, Marius, Macrianus II, Quietus, Florian, Delmatius, and Jovianus. Side by side with the small brass

Fig. 88, Julia Mæsa ; Fig. 89, Julia Mamæa.

Fig. 90, Gordianus Pius ; Fig. 91, Octacilla Severa.

and the washed pieces there was an issue at contemporary dates of coins in pure silver, among the collectable pieces being those of Constans, Julian II, Gratian, Valentinian II, Valens, Honorius, Theodosius, and Arcadius.

Many of the pieces struck just before the fall of the Western Empire of Rome are interesting from the place of their mintage, mostly recorded. Foremost among the mint towns of Byzantine Emperors in the provinces was London (Londinium), where many of the coins of Carausius were struck, about A.D. 291; the abbreviations are "LON.," "LN.," and "AVGOB." Carausius also struck coins at Colchester (Camulodunum), and some of the small coins of Allectus were struck there, too; the marks are "C." and "C.L." Treves (Treveri) was distinguished by "TR." and "TROB.," and was used as a mint in the time of Diocletian, Valens, Gratian, and others. The mint marks of Lyons (Lugdunum) are "L.," "LG.," and "LVG.," and it was a mint much used by Gallienus. Arles was a mint town of Constantine, and its coins may be determined by "AR." or "ARL." The mint marks of Constantinople are "CON," and "CONS." Another important mint was Ravenna, known by "R.," "RV.," or "RAV."

The collector of Roman coins, perhaps more than in any other branch of numismatics, is faced with the numerous counterfeits which have been made; not always modern forgeries, but more frequently those made centuries ago. One of the most noted "duplicators" was Carl Becker, who was born in 1771. His pieces were of good metal and beautifully executed—a little too good, for their superiority of finish gives them away; moreover, they are rather higher in relief than the originals; they are more noticeable, too, in that they chiefly represent very rare coins, and for that reason they are often retained in the cabinet, filling up gaps which would otherwise be vacant. Becker's forgeries include Greek, Roman, and Mediæval.

There are ancient forgeries, too, for many finds of Roman coins in this country include copies made for actual circulation by the British, after the Romans had left our shores. Although forgeries and authorized coins were struck from carefully prepared dies, the duplication of coins was sometimes cheaply effected by casting in clay. The little moulds made of pellets of clay impressed with a coin which had been originally struck from an approved die only lasted two or three times, after which they were thrown away. Being perishable, they are not often found entire, although fragments are commonly met with on the site of such a mint.

Collectors, although probably failing to see anything to admire in the very crude series of coins issued by the Emperors of the Eastern Empire after the downfall of the Western division of the once most powerful nation that the world had known, cannot very well ignore such pieces, as they are able to secure them in good condition. Taking their name from the ancient one of the city of Constantine, the true Byzantium series begins with coins of Anastasius I, A.D. 491–518, and continues until the middle of the fifteenth century, gradually getting merged into the issues of European nations of mediæval days. The dies, even of the earlier pieces of the series, had lost all the beauty of the old Roman currency, and were badly cut and very carelessly designed. It must be remembered, however, that this money coined at Constantinople, Nicomedia, Rome, Carthage, and Alexandria, had a very wide circulation. Many of the places from which it was issued had possessed mints before. Roman varieties of Alexandrian coins with distinct characteristics had been struck there during the reigns of many of the old Emperors, but the new coins were destined to have a large circulation in the Mediterranean and on the Continent of Europe. The follis introduced by Diocletian had reached its height in the reign of Justinian; its nominal value was then 40 noumia, and the mark appearing in the centre of the reverse was the Greek numeral M. Chief among its subdivisions was the half-value piece, marked by the Greek K or the Roman numerals XX (twenty); its lesser parts being similarly distinguished.

The crude lettering of the inscriptions on these coins is not always easy to trace; on those of Anastasius it generally takes the form of "D.N.ANASTASIVS PP.AVG." (Our Lord Anastasius, Perpetual Augustus.) A common feature in this coinage is the frequency of two figures side by side, notably in the reign of Phocas. When we reach the ninth century most of the inscriptions are found across the field in two or three lines: thus a coin of Theophilus, A.D. 829, reads on the reverse, "THEOFILEAVS OVSTASV NICAS."

A coin of Basil I reads in badly formed Greek letters, when translated, "Basil and Constantine, by the Grace of God, Kings of the Romans." This pious legend of the ninth century is used to-day on the coins of Christian kings, in Latin form, for in the words "Dei Gratia" we still acknowledge the Divine Protector and maker of kings.

Among the coins of this period are those of Romanus and Leo and a few others, uninteresting, but necessary in order to make such a collection complete. Lastly, the series of Byzantine coins includes the curious twelfth-century cup-shaped pieces minted in all metals; they are concave on the obverse and convex on the reverse. Essentially religious in their design the obverse represents the King in the act of being crowned by the Virgin Mary, and on the reverse Jesus Christ enthroned. The legends are very indistinct, but "I.C." in the field by the side of the head of our Saviour, are letters readily deciphered.

VII

EARLY BRITISH AND ROMANO-BRITISH

CHAPTER VII

EARLY BRITISH AND ROMANO-BRITISH

The British currency before the landing of the Romans—The coinage of Imperial money in Britain, and of the continuance of its use after the evacuation of this country by the Romans.

RECORDS of the earliest coined money used in Britain are wrapped in tradition and conjecture. It is, however, generally acknowledged that the Britons who dwelt in these islands before the first Roman invasion had a metallic currency. The British gold stater has been found under conditions which can leave no doubt as to its authentic use as money, and as a British coin. It was, undoubtedly, modelled from the design of the beautiful gold coins of Philip II of Macedon, whose staters not only circulated in Greece and her colonies, but were very generally employed among the more civilized peoples in other parts of Europe. These staters were copied by the Gauls who received them from Marseilles, then the Greek colony of Massilia ; and the Gaulish traders who came to Britain brought over local imitations from which it is thought most of the early British coins were copied, rather than from Philip of Macedon's original staters.

There may, however, have been British mints of still earlier date, for it is probable that the idea of minting coins of more convenient form than the native ring money, some of which has been found in Ireland and in Celtic British graves, occurred to Britishers before they had seen the coinage of other nations. Sir John Evans, the great authority on this series, places the first British mint in Kent as early as B.C. 150. Such coins are designated (1) uninscribed, that is without any lettered inscriptions upon them, and (2) inscribed, that is with a lettered inscription added to one or other of the different devices. Uninscribed coins of gold and silver, and in a few instances of copper and mixed metals, are met with. The general type is that of a rudely engraved head, based on a crude copy of the stater. The reverse is an equally poor representation of a horse, of the triple-tailed type, in the field being numerous pellets. Some of the examples, especially those included in an important find at Freckenham, in 1885, are said to have been minted by the Iceni; many similar pieces have been found in the Channel Islands. That given in Fig. 93 shows the triple-tailed horse and a chariot-wheel on the reverse.

The inscribed coins bear different letterings, which, with more or less uncertainty, have been accorded to British chieftains, the actual dates of issue in most cases being somewhat uncertain. Among the inscibed series better authenticated than many others are those of Cunobeline, of which there are specimens in all metals. His gold coins are generally inscribed on the obverse, "CAMVL," and the silver and copper

Fig. 92, Eighth-century Sceatta ; Fig. 93, Early British coin ;
Fig. 94, Coin of Tasciovanus.

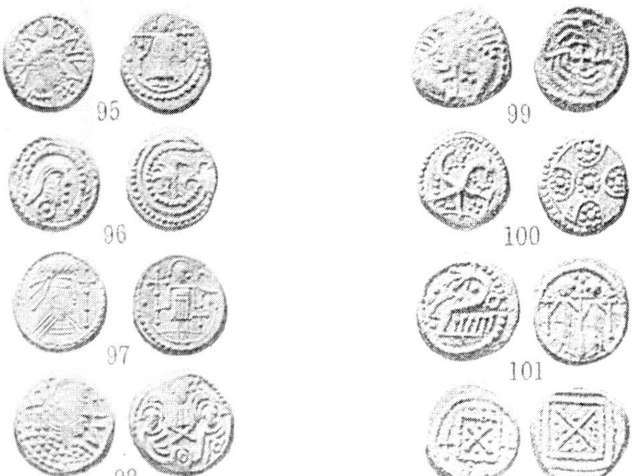

Figs. 95–102, Saxon Sceattas of various types.

"CVNO," in some instances the name reading in full. On these are emblems such as a bull or a horse; in one instance Vulcan is represented forging a helmet. The coins of Tasciovanus are not uncommon, and may be readily recognized by their inscriptions, which, although varied, usually read, "TASC." Fig. 94 is a copper coin of this prince minted at Verulamium, inscribed. Other similar pieces are ascribed respectively to Eppillus, Comux, Antedrigus, Verica, and Tincommius.

When the Romans came to Britain they found these scanty currencies insufficient for their purposes of trade, and gradually introduced a supplementary currency of Roman coins minted in Britain, although they brought over with them a plentiful supply of Imperial currency for the payment of troops, according to their custom. The Romans maintained settlements, and more or less intermittently occupied the towns they had built, and the camps they had fortified, for centuries.

In order to understand the Roman coins having reference to the occupation of Britain by the Imperial troops, and to account for the immense quantities of Roman gold, silver, and bronze, which have been found in Britain, it is necessary to trace the connection with the Emperors of Rome and their northern Province. Britain, also called Albion, was unknown to the Romans until Julius Cæsar crossed over from a place of embarkation between Calais and Boulogne, to invade it. That was in the autumn of the year B.C. 55, when he landed on the Kentish shore with a small force. The following year he again invaded these islands, and landed with five legions, gaining control over Essex and Middlesex, afterwards making peace with the natives on their agreeing to the payment of an annual tribute. Claudius Cæsar, about A.D. 50, undertook the further subjugation of the country, and his troops were kept moving about, one notable event being the capture of the Isle of Anglesea, when many Druid priests were killed. Then followed the massacre of the Romans by the Britons under their enraged Queen, Boadicea, in A.D. 61.

In another expedition Vespasian obtained a stronger hold of Britain, and, later, the Romans under the command of Agricola, A.D. 78, brought the greater part of the island under their power. During the reigns of the earlier Emperors no special reference to Britain is met with on the coins left behind by the Roman troops. Hadrian who landed in person on British ground, A.D. 121, minted coins bearing upon them allusions to his conquest. Under Septimus Severus, the island was divided into two sections under able governors, but from the death of Severus to the beginning of the reign of the usurper Carausius, there is little of note to record in connection with the Romans in Britain. As already stated in an earlier chapter it is, however, to the Romans that we owe the figure of our well-known national emblem—Britannia.

Carausius, who was a military commander sent out by the Romans with a naval force to check the outrages of pirates on the coasts of Holland, France, and Spain, having incurred the displeasure of his Imperial

Figs. 103 and 104, Coins of Offa ; Fig. 105, Cynethryth ;
Fig. 106, Coenwulf.

Fig. 107, Ceolwulf I ; Fig. 108, Beornwulf.

Fig. 109, Eadberht II , Fig. 110, Baldred

Sovereign, crossed over to Britain, and was favourably received by the Roman troops there stationed. In A.D. 287 he was made ruler of Britain by the soldiers, with the title of Augustus. For several years his fleets swept the seas, and commanded the mouths of the Rhine and the Seine, during which time coins were minted in this country, and undoubtedly formed a part of the British currency, and may well be included in a cabinet of coins relating to Britain. Of these there are many varieties, both in silver and bronze, the "third brass" reverses being unusually numerous.

On the death of Carausius, Allectus, who was the assassinator of the king whose friend he had been, was declared his successor in A.D. 293. His coins are not so numerous as those of Carausius; a few are found, however, with the coins of the Constantines, which are plentiful in Britain. Constantius Chlorus, who crossed over from Gaul and marched against Allectus, seems to have brought with him much money for the payment of troops, and, in addition, a mint was set up in London. Although the Romans finally left Britain early in the fifth century of the Christian era, their coins were in current use by the natives until the more settled times of the Saxon period.

VIII

THE SAXON PERIOD

CHAPTER VIII

THE SAXON PERIOD

Early imitations of Roman money—The sceattas of the Saxons—The first penny struck by Offa—The last coins of the period issued by Harold II.

BEFORE the Saxon period commenced the natives of South Britain attempted an imitation of Roman coins, with the view of instituting a coinage of their own, or, perhaps, of supplementing those then in circulation, possibly in some districts insufficient. It is difficult to distinguish between what may be termed local contemporary forgeries of Roman coins and the crude imitations which were evidently the work of authorized die-sinkers in the sixth and seventh centuries. Many such pieces are met with, but they are rarely found in quantities. The genuine Roman coins, on the other hand, have been found in vessels of pottery intact and unbroken, thousands at a time, giving every indication of having been purposely buried by their possessors.

The first definite currency which comes as the connecting link between the Roman and the Anglo-Saxon periods consists of sceattas, an authorized currency mentioned in the laws of Æthelstan, in which it was stated "30,000 sceattas were equal to £120." Thus one of these coins was only a trifle less in value than a penny (see Fig. 92). Apparently the sceattas were designed after the fashion of a contemporary late Roman or Byzantine coin, and were struck chiefly in gold and silver, many of them being now almost undecipherable, and apparently without inscriptions. Some, however, have Christian symbols upon them, others the figure of a wolf, and yet others a few letters, which may possibly be an abbreviation of the name of Æthelbert, King of Kent. It is thought that some of these were struck at Winchester.

Among the obvious copies of Roman coins are those on which the figure of Victory is conspicuous —although crudely executed. The examples given here have been selected to show a variety of types. On the obverse of Fig. 95 is a diademed bust, around it in blundered form "LVNDONIA." There is a curious beaded curve around the head on the obverse of Fig. 96; on the reverse a bird. Fig. 97 is a coin from a better die, and more regularly struck—the figure on the reverse holding a cross in one hand and a bird in the other. The gold sceatta, or triens, illustrated in Fig. 98, is less distinguishable, although the two figures on the reverse are not difficult to trace. On the obverse of Fig. 99 is a cross, on the reverse birds. In the centre of Fig. 100 is a bird on the obverse, and a cross, with rosette in the angles and centre, on the reverse. The types of Fig. 101 are a dragon on the obverse and two figures on the

Fig. 111, Æthelstan I ; Fig. 112, St. Eadmund ; Fig. 113, Jaenberht ; Fig. 114, Wulfred.

Figs. 115 and 116, Ceolnoth ; Fig. 117, Plegmund ; Fig. 118, Æthelstan II.

reverse. Fig. 102 is a less common variety, the type being squares and compartments.

The kingdoms of the Heptarchy were those countries generally defined as Kent, Mercia, East Anglia, Northumbria, and Wessex; and the coins circulating in them are generally placed by collectors in separate groups, in that there are certain peculiarities which distinguish them from others of the series. The coins of Kent are both regal and ecclesiastical. The first group commences with Ecgberht (765–791), in whose reign silver pennies were struck with the king's name on the obverse; on the reverse a cross, in the angles of which are the letters "BABBA." These were followed by an issue of Eadberht II (796–798), his pennies being inscribed on the obverse "EADBEARHT REX," in three lines across the field; on the reverse is the moneyer's name (see Fig. 109). There are coins of Cuthred (798–806) and of Baldred (806–825) (see Fig. 110). The present values of the coins of the foregoing reigns are, unfortunately, high.

The regal coins of Mercia extend from Peada (655–657) onward. Æthelred I, along with Peada, issued sceattas, all of which are rare. There were several very interesting issues during the long reign of Offa (757–796), and his coins are comparatively numerous; one of these is illustrated in Fig. 103. On it may be seen the king's name and title, "OFFA REX"; on the reverse the moneyer's name in the angles of a cross-crosslet, in the centre being a small cross. At that time the king's royal seat was at Kingsbury-on-the-Thame, where he had obtained the services of Italian die-sinkers. He had also mints at

Tamworth, Warwick, and Coventry; the two former were then known respectively as "Tornei" and "Weric." On some of these coins, instead of the king's head, there is the letter "N." Fig. 104 is the usual type without the king's bust, having his name and title in three lines. There are some rare pieces attributed to Cynethryth, the Queen of Offa; one of these is illustrated in Fig. 105. In the reign of Offa the best period of early Saxon mintage was reached.

The next coins are those of Coenwulf (St. Kynwulf), 796–822. A fine example of this reign is given in Fig. 106: on the obverse a bust with radiated hair, the title reading "COENVVLF REX"; on the reverse a cross-crosslet in the centre of a circle. Fig. 107 represents a penny of Ceolwulf (822–823), and Fig. 108 one of Beornwulf (823–825). Other coins of this series are those of Wiglaf (825–839), Berhtulf (839–853), Burgred (853–874), and Ceolwulf II (874–877).

The coins of the East Angles were regal and semi-ecclesiastical. The first of the regal series was a styca of copper of Beonna (760); on this little coin the king's name, in Runic letters, appears on the obverse; on the reverse a cross, in the angles of which are the moneyer's initials (see Figs. 119 and 120). Æthelberht (794) issued a silver sceatta, on which was the king's bust diademed, surrounded by his name; on the reverse the legendary symbol of the wolf and twins, copied from early Roman "brass." The later coins of the East Angles were silver pennies, the first being that of Eadwald (819–827), followed by Æthelstan I (828–837), on some of whose

Figs. 119 and 120, Stycas of the East Angles; Figs. 121–124, Stycas of Northumbria.

DANO-NORSE PENNIES.

Fig. 125, Siefred; Fig. 126, Anlaf; Figs. 127 and 128, York Pennies (St. Peter).

coins may be traced the king's name and title, surrounding his bust, the inscription reading "EDELSTAN REX"; on the reverse, a cross-crosslet in the centre of a circle, surrounded by the moneyer's name. Fig. 111 is another type of penny of Æthelstan I, the inscription reading in four lines on the reverse. Other pennies of this series are those of Æthelweard (837–850), Beorhtric (852), and Æthelstan II (878–890). To these must be added the semi-ecclesiastical coins of St. Eadmund. The penny of St. Eadmund, illustrated in Fig. 112, is without bust, there being a cross-crosslet on the obverse; on the reverse a cross within a beaded circle, a single pellet in each of the angles.

To many there is an especial interest in the ecclesiastical series of pennies, further examples of which are given in Figs. 114 to 118. Fig. 113 is a penny of Jaenberht, Archbishop of Canterbury (766–790). In Fig. 114 is seen a penny of Wulfred (805–832); this piece, illustrated in *Ruding*, is described as "a full-faced bust with tonsured head." An exceptionally fine piece of Ceolnoth (833–870) is given in Fig. 115; in the angles of the cross on the reverse may be traced the letters "CIVITAS." A penny of Ceolnoth is given in Fig. 116. There are also pennies of Plegmund (890–914), one of which is shown in Fig. 117, the latter being very rare. Fig. 118 is a penny of Æthelstan II.

The Northumbrian coins are all stycas, for the most part copper, although some are base silver (see Figs. 121–124). The regal stycas extend from 670–900. Of these there are many varieties known, the commoner pieces, easily collectable, being those of Eanred, Æthelred, and Redwulf. To take these in rotation, the collection may be arranged as follows: Ecgfrith (670–685), copper; Aldfrid (685–705), silver; Eadberht (737–758), base silver (see Fig. 122); Alchred (765–774), silver; Osred II (788–790), copper; Eardwulf (796–806), copper; Eanred (807–841), silver and copper; Redwulf (844), copper; Osberht (849–867), copper; and Æthelred II (841–849), one of whose copper stycas is illustrated in Fig. 123. From this piece some idea of the style of lettering of the stycas of that period may be gathered. This coin reads "EDILRED REX" on the obverse; and on the reverse is the moneyer's name, with a small cross-crosslet in the centre.

After the coins of Northumbria came the Dano-Norse silver pennies. The different chieftains of whom there are coins are: Earl Sihtric (871); Halfdan (876–877); Guthred (877–894); Siefred (894–898), see Fig. 125 (there is also a silver half-penny of this reign); Aldwald (901–905); Regnald (943–944); Anlaf (941–952) (see Fig. 126); and Eric (948–954).

The coinage of Wessex includes some of the more important reigns, notably those of Æthelred I and Alfred the Great. The whole of the coins of this kingdom were then silver—pennies and half-pennies. They circulated from the Thames to the Firth of Forth, the Wessex Kingdom being afterwards merged in the currency of the sole monarchs. The coins of Ecgberht (802–839) have upon their obverses the bust of the king, with his superscription; on the reverse a cross, and in some cases the monogram of the City of Canterbury. The illustration given in Fig. 129 is without bust or mint name. Many of the pennies of Æthelwulf (839–858) have upon their reverses the Christian monogram; others have only a simple cross (see Fig. 130). There are pennies of Æthelbald (856–861), which are very rare; and scarcely so are those of Æthelbearht (858–866). On the other hand, the pennies of Æthelred I (863–871) are fairly common.

The long reign of Alfred the Great (871–901) marked an important epoch in British history. Many various types of coins were issued, the chief mints being Oxford and London. Other coins were struck at Canterbury, Exeter, Gloucester, and Winchester. Of most of those mints there are both pennies and half-pennies, examples of King Alfred's pennies being shown in Figs. 131 and 132. The remaining coins of the Kings of Wessex are those of Eadweard the Elder (901–925), pennies and half-pennies; Athelstan (925–941), pennies; Eadmund (941–946), pennies; Eadred (946–955), pennies and half-pennies; and Eadwig (955–959) pennies.

In connection with the moneys of the West Saxons it is interesting to note the origin of the term "Peter's Pence." Ina, King of the West Saxons, had made a pilgrimage to Rome in the eighth century, and on his return arranged a grant to support an English school or college in the Imperial City. The grant was confirmed by Offa, and to raise the money a tax of one silver penny was levied on every householder whose yearly possessions amounted to thirty pence as an annual value. The only exception made to the payment of St. Peter's pence was that of the Abbey and tenants of the abbey lands of St. Albans. It is said that in later years the Popes appropriated the donation to their own uses. Payments, therefore, were forbidden by Edward III, in 1366, although there were later attempts to revive the custom. In this connection it has sometimes been erroneously stated that a coin was specially struck for payment of this tax. The coin so referred to was a very interesting penny struck in York, then in the Kingdom of Northumbria, the issue being in the tenth century, when the Archbishops of York had an important mint, described in the old form on the coins as Ebracei (Eboracum); on the obverse the legend reads, "SCI. PETR. MO." (see Figs. 127 and 128).

The coins of the sole monarchs of England bring us to a more interesting period, commencing as it does with the coins of Eadgar (957–975), who was the last Anglo-Saxon king to strike coins without mint names. Eadgar established uniformity of the currency; of his coins, however, there are several varieties—some with, some without, the bust, several being very scarce. Eadweard II, better known as Edward the Martyr (975–979), struck many coins, mostly of rude types; on these his title appears as "REX ANGLORVM" (King of England). There are several pennies of Æthelred II (979–1016), one variety of which is shown in Fig. 135. On it the King is represented in a kind of mailed armour peculiar to that period, and wearing a crowned

WESSEX PENNIES.

Fig. 129, Ecgberht ; Fig. 130, Æthelwulf ; Figs. 131 and 132, Alfred the Great.

SAXON SOLE MONARCHS.

Fig. 133, Harold I ; Fig. 134, Harold II ; Fig. 135, Æthelred II ; Fig. 136, Edward the Confessor.

helmet. This issue is interesting, as it was at that time that the voided cross was introduced. On some of Æthelred II's coins will be noticed a sceptre, an emblem of sovereignty which then appeared for the first time on British coins.

One of the most prolific reigns of the Anglo-Saxon period is that of Cnut (1016–1035), there being no less than 340 variations of the moneyers' names. At this period the letters "PACX" in the angles of a voided cross are seen for the first time. They were instituted to denote the peace established with Eadmund Ironside in 1016. This type of obverse was a favourite one with the issuers of Saxon and Early Norman coins. There are no coins of Eadmund Ironside, the son of Æthelred. One of the pennies of Harold I (1035–1040) is illustrated in Fig. 133. There are some of Harthacnut (1040–1042), but most of them appear to have been minted in Denmark.

Then followed Edward the Confessor (1042–1066), whose coins are numerous (see Fig. 136). The last Anglo-Saxon king was Harold II, who perished at the Battle of Hastings. This prince, looked upon by many as a usurper, had married the daughter of Earl Godwin. He had also some claim to the crown through the Danish line. The silver pennies of Harold are of the "Pax" type, and for the most part scarce (see Fig. 134). With his reign the series of Saxon coins came to an end.

IX

NORMAN AND PLANTAGENET

CHAPTER IX

NORMAN AND PLANTAGENET

Money of account—Many mint towns—The gold coins of Edward III —Anglo-Gallic coins

AFTER the conquest of England by William the Norman, when he had taken possession of the chief towns, and a settlement of the country had been partially effected, fresh coins were issued. There was no material change in their designs, which followed closely those of the Anglo-Saxon kings, and were similar to the silver then circulating in Normandy. The gold bezants of Constantinople were used by most Continental nations, and circulated in this country too, but the only silver currency was the penny and its divisional parts. Some changes, however, were made in the fictitious denominations of currency, or, as they are often termed, "imaginary coins." Of these there was the *mark*—a Danish computation, introduced about the time of Alfred the Great, superseded to some extent in the time of William by the *shilling*, which was then only a coin of account of the nominal value of twelve pennies. The mark, then used in a similar way, was computed at 160 pennies. Some confusion has been caused by the term "sterling," which was early connected with our coinage. It applied to the quality of the mintage, which was examined periodically at Easter. Hence, the term "Easterling" or "sterling" denoted coins of true weight and value as last attested.

William I (1066–1087).

The pennies of William weighed from 20 to 21 grains, and there were farthings and half-pennies as money of account, but not then struck as separate coins, the penny being broken in two or four along the arms of the cross on the reverse, for use as might be most convenient. The name of "Willeem" is spelt on the coins with a Saxon "P" instead of "W," hence the reading of the legend, "PILLEEM REX," sometimes spelt "PILLELM REX." It is said there are upwards of 250 moneyers' names, spelt in different ways, attributable to this reign, and upwards of sixty mints. Of the chief types of the obverses are those with the king's profile bust to left with sceptre, and the "bonnet" type—a front face with crown and tassels, the latter as shown on the illustration, Fig. 137, which also represents the king holding a sceptre. The common type of the reverse is the PAXS type, the letters being in the angles of the cross on the reverse. A specimen from the Exeter Mint is given in Fig. 138.

William II (1087–1100).

There appear to be very few distinguishing marks between the pennies of William II and those of his

Figs. 137 and 138, William I Pennies ; Figs. 139 and 140, Henry I Pennies.

Fig. 141, Henry I Penny ; Figs. 142 and 143, Stephen ; Fig. 144, Edward I.

father. It is surmised, therefore, that comparatively few coins were struck during the time of William Rufus, and that the greater part of those issued were from the dies used in the previous reign. Usually the pennies of William II, actually struck during his reign, and especially the latter part of it, are slightly heavier than those of the Conqueror, weighing over 21 grains. The principal varieties of the coins, which do not in their inscriptions on the obverse differ materially, are a full front face with a star at either side, and a front face with a sword instead of a sceptre. Another scarcer variety has a front face with sceptre, and a star at the left side of the head. The inscriptions on all these usually read "PILLEEM REX."

Henry I (1100–1135).

Most of the pennies of this reign are somewhat cruder in form and not so clearly cut as the early pennies of the Anglo-Norman period. Henry seems to have recognized the necessity of preventing forgery and clipping coins; and heavy penalties, such as the loss of a hand, were inflicted. Many of the moneyers who had apparently reduced the size of the coins were executed.

There are several points of difference besides the change of name, which make it comparatively easy to distinguish between the pennies of Henry I and those of his predecessors, although the king's name is spelt in various ways. In some cases only the initials "H. R." are found; on others the full name HENRICVS," to which is added "REX," or "REX

ANGLORVM." Of the several varieties there are front-faced coins similar to those of William, on the reverse a cross fleury with trefoil in each angle, and reverses with "PAX" across the field; some with profile of large size, a sceptre in the right hand; and on others a full front or three-quarter face with sceptre on the obverse and cross fleury on the reverse. There are many names of moneyers, and upwards of thirty mints are mentioned. For example of Henry I's pennies, see Figs. 139–141.

Stephen (1135–1154).

The coins of Stephen are much scarcer than those of his predecessor, with whom, it will be remembered, the male line of the Normans became extinct. Stephen was descended from the fourth daughter of the Conqueror, usurping the crown to the prejudice of Maud, the only surviving child of Henry I. During the reign of Stephen much debased money was minted, very many earls and barons issuing pieces from which they gained some profit. In 1153 the Treaty of Wallingford abolished the illegal mints, which, however, continued to be used during the greater portion of Stephen's reign. For the most part all these illegal coins or tokens were badly struck, and many of them are of light weight and of somewhat irregular sizes.

Two exceptionally fine examples of Stephen's coins are illustrated in Figs. 142 and 143, on which the king, crowned, is represented holding a sceptre. The king's name is spelt in several ways on his coins; sometimes as in the illustration, at others abbreviated, reading frequently "STEINE." There were about twenty-seven lawful mints in addition to those of the barons.

During Stephen's reign some ecclesiastical pennies were minted by Henry, Bishop of Winchester, a younger brother of the king; on the obverse is the bishop's head with a crozier in the front, surrounded by the inscription, "HENRICVS EPC," on the reverse "STEPHANVS REX." There are also some pieces which purport to have upon them representations of Stephen and Matilda his wife, it being conjectured that they were struck at a time when Matilda commanded the army during the trouble with the Barons in 1141. Coins were also issued at York by Eustace, an elder son of Stephen, these being of small weight, about 16 grains. William, a second son of Stephen, is said to have struck coins at Chichester and at Wisbeach, this prince marrying Isabel, the daughter of the then Earl of Surrey and Lord of Wisbeach. Robert, Earl of Gloucester, who was an illegitimate son of Henry I, who had commanded the forces of Matilda when she took up arms against Stephen, on behalf of her son, struck some silver pennies, all of which are now rare. Coins were also struck at Bristol, Lincoln, and Warwick, by Roger, Earl of Warwick.

Henry II (1154–1189).

Henry Plantagenet, the son of Maud, inherited lands in Normandy from his mother, and after his marriage annexed the Duchy of Aquitaine, in France. The coins of Henry II were of two distinct types. The first issue, struck in 1156, were very irregular in shape, and difficult to decipher; the coins of the second issue were more regular, and were of what is known as the short-cross type. On the first issue the king's bust is nearly full face; he holds a sceptre in his right hand, and on the reverse in the angles of the cross are usually small crosses. The second issue has the king's head within an inner circle, on the reverse a double-barrelled cross. On these coins the names of many mint towns, chiefly in abbreviated form, may be deciphered. The coins of the last issue are now by far the commonest.

Richard I (1189–1199), and John (1199–1216).

There are no English coins with the name of Richard I on them. Apparently those struck during Richard's reign were from the dies used by his father. There are, however, Continental coins on which Richard is described as Duke of Aquitaine.

During the reign of John no English pennies were issued under his own name, although there are Irish coins on which he is described as the Lord of Ireland, (see Chapter XVIII). There are a few rare half-pennies issued from the London and Winchester Mints, on the obverses of which there is the king's head to right, and the legend "IOHANNES."

Henry III (1216–1272).

The reign of Henry III is notable for the introduction of a gold coinage. A gold penny was struck, ordered to pass current at the rate of twenty silver pennies ; it is said that it was not popular, and was soon reduced in value and ultimately called in. On the obverse of this remarkable coin, which did not meet with the approval of British traders, the king was represented sitting on a throne ; on the reverse a double cross with a rose in each angle.

The silver currency of Henry III consisted of two issues, the first of the type of Henry II's issue, the second, the head of the king, front face. On the reverse was a short double cross with three pellets in each angle, a device which was retained for a great number of years on this silver coinage.

Edward I (1272–1307), and Edward II (1307–1327).

No gold was struck during these reigns. The silver coins, however, were increased by the addition of a farthing, the three values being issued from many different mints, notably London, Lincoln, Bristol, Exeter, Durham, Canterbury, Reading, Berwick, and York. There was a pattern groat issued in very small quantities, but it does not appear to have been put in circulation (see Fig. 149). Collectors experience great difficulty in distinguishing the silver coins of the first three Edwards, as no numerals were used after the name. Several schemes have been suggested by which the separate issues can be distinguished, one is that the coins of Edward I are almost invariably inscribed in abbreviated form "EDW." Those of Edward II have usually the addition of one or more letters, whereas the coins of Edward III were inscribed in full, "EDWARDVS." The weight of the penny at that time was 22½ grains; and it may be mentioned that the weights of the early silver coins should be carefully noted, as they often help a collector to determine the age or issue of a specimen. The coins of Berwick have often a curious and interesting mint mark on the reverse, that of two bears' head.

Edward III (1327–1377).

The reign of Edward III marks the commencement of a more interesting period in the coins of this country, for it was then that an extended coinage was issued, including gold nobles, the issue of which commenced in the fourteenth year of the king's reign. They were truly noble coins, their value being affixed at six shillings and eightpence sterling. Describing the obverse of the general type of gold noble (see Figs. 145 and 148), it may be briefly given as a ship of the period, on which was a streamer at the mast-head bearing the Cross of St. George, and represented, on a very large scale of drawing, the king standing, holding a drawn sword in his right hand, and on his left arm a pointed shield held askew, on the shield being quartered the arms of England and those of France. Caxton writing of this currency says: "Edward in his fourteenth year commanded his coin of gold to be made forthwith. The best that might be, that is to say, the florin that was called the noble." This new coin was made current by proclamation. An important distinguishing mark on the reverse of the

Fig. 149, Edward I Groat; Fig. 150, Richard II Half-groat; Fig. 151, Henry IV Groat.

Fig. 152, Edward IV Half-rose-noble; Fig. 153, Henry VI Quarter-noble; Fig. 154, Edward V Angel.

noble, in the centre of the four-armed cross, is a rose of four petals, in the middle the letter "E."

In addition to the gold nobles there are florins, half-florins, and quarter-florins, and half-nobles (see Fig. 147), and quarter-nobles (see Fig. 146). The nobles of the first issue weighed $138\frac{6}{13}$ grains; the second issue 128 grains, and the third issue $120\frac{4}{7}$ grains. The first issue may be distinguished by the letter "L" for London in the centre of the cross on the reverse. On the second issue the central letter is "E" for Edward. The third issue is divided into three different periods; in the first, 1351–1360, the title of "King of France" is added to that of King of England; in the second, 1360–1369, the title of "Duke of Aquitaine" is used instead of that of "King of France"; in the last period, 1369–1377, both titles are used. The nobles struck at Calais have the letter "C" in the centre of the cross on the reverse. All these beautiful coins were of 23 carats $3\frac{1}{2}$ grains of pure gold, and only $\frac{1}{2}$ grain alloy.

The introduction of the groat as a common coin of currency in the reign of Edward III adds to the interest of a cabinet of English silver, for it gives the collector a larger and a more imposing piece than had hitherto been used in this country. At that time much black money from Continental mints was used in England, and the impetus to trade which was then being experienced made it necessary that a coin of higher value than the silver penny should be brought into being. The mint towns at that time were London, York, Durham, and Reading. The groat was supplemented by a half-groat piece, and a plentiful supply of the smaller denominations, penny, half-penny, and farthing, was minted.

Richard II (1377–1399).

The gold currency of Richard II consisted of nobles, half-nobles, and quarter-nobles. The silver, of groat, half-groat, penny, half-penny, and farthing. All these pieces were similar in design to those of his grandfather Edward III, the inscription reading, "RICARD. DI. GRA. REX. ANGL. Z. FRANCIA": in the centre of the gold nobles the capital "R" was used instead of "E." The silver coins of Richard II consisted of groat, half-groat, penny, half-penny, and farthing; they were minted at Durham, London, and York. A half-groat of the York Mint is illustrated in Fig. 150.

ANGLO-GALLIC COINS.

Concurrently with the issue of coins in England, by virtue of their dukedoms in France, English kings minted separate coins for use in those dominions. The issues of such coins had assumed considerable importance in the reign of Edward III. The most exhaustive dissertation upon these pieces is a work published by Andrew Ducarel, LL.D., F.S.A., in 1757, in the form of twelve letters to the members of the Society of Antiquaries of London, accompanied by sixteen large-sized plates illustrating many important pieces. At an earlier date, in the reign of Henry II, derniers were struck for the dukedom of

Aquitaine, which had become a dependency in consequence of his marriage with Eleanor of Aquitaine. Richard I, as Earl of Poitou, and also for the lordship of the Duchy of Aquitaine, struck coins for both places as early as A.D. 1168. In the reign of Edward I Anglo-Gallic coins were issued for Gascony and Aquitaine. These were followed by coins struck by the Black Prince, as Duke of that Principality. It will be remembered that in 1362 Edward III had granted the Black Prince the Principality of Aquitaine and Gascony, with the right of coining both gold and silver. On the coins he issued the inscription usually reads, "PRIMOGENITVS REGIS ANGLIAE ET PRINCEPS AQVITAINE" (The eldest son of the King of England and Prince of Aquitaine). Edward III, however, instituted a somewhat more extensive series of coins specially designed for his French possessions, including the guiennois or Guienne piece in gold, which shows the king standing in armour, the "chaise" on which the king is shown seated, and the "leopard." It was in the same reign that the gold nobles were issued from the Calais Mint.

X

COINS OF THE LANCASTRIAN AND YORKIST KINGS

CHAPTER X

COINS OF THE LANCASTRIAN AND YORKIST KINGS

Difficulty in distinguishing the coins of the Henries—York in the ascendency—The ecclesiastical mint of Durham.

Henry IV (1399–1413).

After Richard II had been compelled to abdicate, Henry, Duke of Lancaster, came to the throne by virtue of his descent from Henry III. As Henry IV, the first of the Lancastrian kings of England issued coins not always easy to distinguish from those of his immediate successors, in that their designs are similar and no numerals are given after the kings' names. The gold coins of the first issue were of the same weights as those of the previous reign, but in 1412 the noble was reduced to 108 grains instead of 120, the previous standard, and the penny from 18 grains to 15 grains. Other denominations were reduced proportionately. On the second issue of nobles and half-nobles the arms of France were represented by three fleurs-de-lis, instead of being as formerly semé.

The silver of Henry IV may be divided into "light" and "heavy" coinage. It consisted of groat, half-groat, penny, and farthing, the mint towns being

Durham, London, and York. Fig. 151 represents a groat of the light coinage minted in London; on the obverse is the king's bust, crowned, facing, within a fleury tressure; on the reverse in the centre angles of the cross, three pellets, and the legend, "CIVITAS LONDON."

Henry V (1413–1422).

As already indicated, there are but small differences between the coins of Henry V and Henry VI. On the nobles of Henry V may generally be seen a mullet, an annulet, or a lis, below or above the king's sword-arm, similar marks being observable on the half-nobles above the shield. Coins were chiefly struck at Durham, London, and York, during the reign of Henry V; those issued from the Calais Mint being distinguishable by an annulet on each side of the king's head. The silver coins, consisting of groat, half-groat, penny, half-penny, and farthing, are also obtainable, and are inscribed with the same mint towns as those of Henry IV.

Henry VI (1422–1461).

The only difference between the gold coins of Henry VI and those of his father and grandfather is found in slightly different marks. Thus, on the half- and quarter-nobles there is an annulet. On some nobles, half-, and quarter-nobles, a rosette and mascle, and on a few pieces a pine-cone and mascle. These marks are met with on coins in several combinations. The place of mintage of gold nobles and half-nobles was Calais; silver coins being struck at

Durham, London, York, and also Calais. The king's bust on the silver currency is almost identical with that of his father. A fine quarter-noble of Henry VI is illustrated in Fig. 153.

Edward IV (1461–1483).

The struggle between the Houses of Lancaster and York is a matter of history. The badges of the adherents to the respective claimants have their bearing upon the emblems by which collectors locate their coins, for from this time onward the rose became a familiar feature on the currency of this country. The first issues of Edward IV were similar to those of his predecessor. The noble, which was then of the weight of 108 grains, was made current for eight shillings and fourpence, the silver remaining 15 grains to the penny. In 1465, however, the old weights were restored, the noble being made 120 grains, and the current value raised to ten shillings; the name was then changed to rose-noble or ryal (royal). In Fig. 152 is illustrated one of these beautiful coins—a half-rose-noble—minted in Bristol; on the obverse, in the waves beneath the vessel, may be seen the mint mark "B." A new coin appeared in Edward IV's reign, taking its name, angel, from the type which is described as the Archangel Michael piercing a dragon through its mouth, the legend on the full angel being, "PER CRVCEM . TVA SALVA NOS XPE . REDEMPT," and on the half-angel, "O CRVX : AVE SPES . VNICA." On the reverses of these coins is a ship in which, instead of a mast, there is a cross surmounting a shield, on which are quartered the arms of England

and France. On the right of the cross, the cross of St. George, is the king's initial letter "E," and on the left the white rose of York.

The silver coins of Edward IV were minted at London, Norwich, York, Canterbury, Coventry, and Bristol. The groat of the first issue was 60 grains, and of the second issue 48 grains. There are also pennies, mostly obtainable in a very poor condition.

A very special feature in the English coinage of this period, which it may be convenient to refer to here, is the issues from the ecclesiastical mints of Canterbury, Durham, and York. Those of Durham are especially interesting in that they are more or less collectable in a continuity of pieces representing the issues made during the episcopates of all the Bishops of Durham, who followed one another in quick succession at that time. Some interesting particulars are given of the privileges of the mint in a work on the subject by Mr. Mark Noble, published in 1780. He places the foundation of the episcopal mint at Durham in the reign of Stephen, asserting that the privilege of placing a distinguishing mint mark was conferred by Edward I. On the pennies of Bishop Kellow, who died in 1316, a pastoral staff is the mint mark, the legend locating the Durham Mint reading, "CIVITAS DVNELM." Bishops Beak and Beaumont followed, putting their family arms on their coins. The arms of Bishop Hatfield, who in the reign of Edward III did likewise, consisted of three lions rampant, a cross-patee being used as a mint mark. Bishop Skirlaw, of Lichfield, was translated to Durham in 1388, his arms, the woven meshes of a sieve, marked his humble origin, of which he was evidently not ashamed—his father was a sieve-maker. During the reigns of the Henries the Bishops of Durham continued to mint coins and to mark them with their emblems. It is said that Bishop Booth "conducted himself with great propriety during the contentions between the Houses of Lancaster and York." His coins are fairly numerous, on the obverse being the letter "B"; that on the reverse being "D"[unelmensis]. That prelate eventually became Archbishop of York. Bishop Dudley marked his coins with a cross and the letter "D."

The Durham Mint retained its popularity in the days of Cardinal Wolsey, and pennies of that period may be distinguished by "T.W." upon them. It was when Henry VIII threw off the power of the Papacy that the ancient privileges of the Bishops of Durham and Ely, and also of the two Archbishops of Canterbury and York, were curtailed, and Durham lost its ecclesiastical mint.

Edward V (April to June, 1483).

There are few coins of Edward V, mostly angels and half-angels in gold, and groats in silver. They are distinguishable only by the mint mark, the boar's head, or the rose and sun united, the badges of the Protector who afterwards became Richard III. In Fig. 154 is given an angel, on both sides of which are the mint marks rose and sun, united.

Richard III (1483–1485).

During the short reign of Richard III angels and

half-angels in gold, and groats, half-groats, pennies, and half-pennies in silver, were struck. The mint marks, then an established feature in English coinage, were the same as on the coins struck during the lifetime of Edward V. Groats were minted in London and York, and half-groats and half-pennies in London only. There are pennies of the London, Durham, and York Mints. Most of the coins of Richard III, whose reign brought to a close another period in English history, are scarce.

XI

THE TUDOR PERIOD

CHAPTER XI

THE TUDOR PERIOD

The first English sovereign—A new silver coin—Debased coinage of Henry VIII—Fine gold piece of Mary—Elizabethan silver.

Henry VII (1485–1509).

There were two issues of gold in the reign of Henry VII, the first of the Tudor Sovereigns. The first issue consisted of nobles or ryals, angels, and half-angels; the second issue of angels and half-angels, and a new gold coin—the first of our English sovereigns. On the obverse of this beautiful new piece the king is represented seated on a canopied throne, holding in his right hand a sceptre, and in his left an orb. Surrounding the piece is the legend, "HENRICVS . DEI . GRA . ANGL . ET . FRAN . DNS . HIBN." On the reverse are the arms of England and France on a shield impaled upon a Tudor rose, the design being no longer that of the cross fleury of the nobles, but taking the form of a tressure of ten arches. The legend, which was somewhat remarkable, surrounding the device was "IHESVS . AVTEM . TRANSIENS : PER : MEDIVM : ILLORVM : IBAT" (*But Jesus passing through the midst of them went His way*—a quotation from Holy Scripture). All the gold of this reign appears to have been issued from the Tower Mint, which was in years to come to be the chief seat of mintage for British coinage.

The silver coinage of Henry VII was at first similar to that of his immediate predecessors, as regards groats, pennies, half-pennies, and farthings; but the shilling or testoon was a new silver coin of some importance. It weighed 144 grains, and presented a true portrait of the king, around whose head was the inscription, and on the reverse the royal arms on a shield (see Fig. 155). There were two distinct issues struck at the various mint towns, which were Canterbury, London, and York, with some few coins issued from Durham. The initials of the bishops and archbishops of the respective sees are found upon those coins issued from the ecclesiastical mints. Thus, the initial letter "M" stands for Archbishop Morton of Canterbury; "T" for Thomas Rotherham, Archbishop of York; and "R. D." for Richard Fox, of Durham; the same letters being used by his successor, Thomas Ruthall, who was bishop of that see 1509–1522.

Fig. 156 represents one of the rarities of English silver; it is a groat of Perkin Warbeck, struck during his insurrection. On the obverse of this scarce piece are the royal arms, crowned, flanked by fleur-de-lis and rose, on the reverse lis and lion. This impostor, who claimed to be the younger of the two Yorkist princes murdered in the Tower by Richard II, was executed in 1499, after a few years' adventurous career.

155 157 156

Fig. 155, Henry VII Shilling; Fig. 156, Perkin Warbeck Groat; Fig. 157, Edward VI Gold Crown.

158

Fig. 158, Mary Sovereign.

Henry VIII (1509–1547).

Henry VIII is known to coin collectors as the bold monarch who tampered with the purity of the English coinage. He debased gold and silver alike, and when once royal avarice had gained the ascendant there seems to have been no limit to the debasement which ensued. The gold currency of England, at first of pure metal, or according to an approved standard, 23 carats 3½ grains fine metal, and ½ grain alloy, was reduced by Henry VIII to 22 carats fine and 2 carats alloy, followed by further debasement of purity and weight. The first issue in 1509 scaled 240 grains, reduced in the third issue of 1543 to 200 grains, further lowered two years later to 192 grains. The first issue represented the king enthroned, a small portcullis, the distinguishing badge of the Tudors, being added. The second issue may be recognized by the mint marks, which on the obverse was a lily, and on the reverse an arrow. In the third issue the Arabic numeral "8" was used instead of the Roman "VIII."

In addition to the sovereign, half-sovereign, and quarter-angel, two new coins were introduced in the reign of Henry VIII; the one named a crown was equivalent to a quarter-sovereign. In the second issue the sovereign was reduced to 57 grains, in the fourth and fifth issues to 48 grains; on the obverse of these pieces there is the double rose, crowned, the letters "H I" (or "H R") on either side of the field, the legend reading "HENRIC. VIII. RVTILANS: ROSA: SIE (*Sine*) SPIA. (*Spina*)"; on the reverse is a shield of arms, crowned, with the royal initials, crowned, in the field as on the obverse. There were five issues of silver, the first of which resembled those of Henry VII, the only difference being the change in the numerals from "VII" to "VIII." On the second coinage there is a likeness of the king in profile, showing him younger and more corpulent than his father. The half-groat was similar; on those coins issued at the York Mint were the initials of Wolsey, and the Cardinal's hat as a mint mark. The small denominations of that issue were of several types, the penny having for its obverse the king seated on a throne.

The third coinage of Henry VIII's reign marked a period of depreciation in the quality of the metal, and a considerable increase in the alloy used. The king is shown with a three-quarter face bust on the obverse; on the reverse there are a crown and a large rose, around them the old motto: "POSVI: DEV: ADIVTOREM: MEVM." The groats and smaller pieces were coined in the older type of reverse. The types of the fourth coinage were similar but still further debased in quality. The fifth issue of groats was even more copper-like, being merely washed with silver. The chief mints of Henry VIII, in addition to London, were Bristol, Canterbury, Durham, and York.

Edward VI (1547–1553).

In the first year of the reign of Edward VI, this young prince, only nine years old, commenced keeping a journal, and it is said among the important entries in the earlier portions was that declaring a determination to improve the debased coinage then in circulation. The early coins, however, were poor in quality. The first issue of gold consisted of half-sovereign, crown (see Fig. 157), and half-crown, minted in 1547. To these in the second issue were added a sovereign and treble-sovereign, and in the third issue in 1549 a double-sovereign, an angel and half-angel. The first serious attempt to improve the quality of the gold was made in the second issue when the standard was raised to 22 carats, but the weight was reduced. In the third issue, however, the old standard was revived, and the sovereign once more weighed 240 grains, and was of 23 carats 3½ grains fine, and ½ grain alloy. The angel was then made current for eight shillings.

There were three issues of silver during the short reign of Edward VI, the first in 1547 consisting of groat, half-groat, penny, and half-penny, the standard being of the impoverished quality used at the end of the reign of Henry VIII. In 1549 there was an issue of shillings struck at Bristol, London, and Southwark Mints. These are interesting in that this was the first issue on which dates were placed on English silver coins. On the obverse was a profile bust of the king crowned; on the reverse an oval shield of arms, the legend reading: "TIMOR. DOMINI. FONS. VITAE" (*The fear of the Lord is the fountain of life*). This is followed by the date, "MDXLII." The most striking addition to the collector's cabinet of English silver is that splendid series of large crown pieces commencing with the silver crown of Edward VI, which is met with dated 1551, 1552, or 1553. In the centre of the obverse is the king, crowned, riding on a horse, fully apparelled, the date under the horse, the legend around it reading: "EDWARD. VI : D : G : ANG : FRA : Z : HIBE : REX :" On the reverse is a shield of arms on a cross, around it the legend "POSVI. DEVM. ADIVTOREM. MEVM." The shilling of the fifth year was made heavier, being increased to 96 grains, and on the side of the full-faced bust, crowned, are the numerals "XII," for twelve pence, on the reverse a square shield of arms on a cross. The small coins of this reign are interesting: a sixpence was struck in the fifth year, weighing 48 grains, similar to the shilling in its design, but differing in the inscription and the denomination, which was "VI." Among the debased coins of the first issue were groats and threepences which were struck in the fifth year, similar to the sixpence, but with "III," for threepence at the side of the head. Half-groats were minted at Canterbury and London in the first year, and there were also pennies minted at Bristol and London. Specimens of the former mint are now rare. There were also half-pennies and farthings. Among the different mint marks met with is an ostrich's head, the crest of Sir Edmund Peckham, the Lord High Treasurer of the Mint; the coins with a "Y" for a mint mark just over the king's crown, stand for Sir John Yorke, who was the mint-master at Southwark, where the crown piece was coined.

Mary (1553–1554), and Philip and Mary (1554–1558).

Mary succeeded to the English throne on the death of the young king, and the following year married

Philip of Spain. This accounts for some of her coins having upon them the duplex title, and the heads of both Sovereigns. The standard of gold coins issued shortly after Queen Mary's accession was raised to 23 carats 3½ grains, fine gold; but her silver was debased. The sovereign, a very fine example of which is illustrated in Fig. 158, shows a striking similarity to the sovereign of Henry VII. On this fine piece the queen is represented enthroned, holding the sceptre in her right hand and the orb in her left. At her feet is the Westminster portcullis; and after her name a small pomegranate, the badge of her mother, Catherine of Aragon. The coin is dated after the royal legend. The reverse shows a shield of arms in the centre of a double rose within an arched tressure. The motto reads: "A : DNO : FACTV : EST ISTV. ET EST MIRA : IN : OCVL : NRIS" (*It is the work of the Lord, and it is wonderful in our eyes*).

Mary also coined ryals of 120 grains, and angels of 80 grains. Her silver before her marriage consisted of groat, half-groat, and penny. On the obverse was the queen's profile with title, and on the reverse, surrounding the arms, "VERITAS TEMP FILIA" (*Truth is the daughter of Time*).

The only gold coins of Philip and Mary were the angel and half-angel of the type of the Archangel St. Michael slaying the dragon. The legend on these pieces is: "PHILIP : Z : MARIA : D : G : REX : Z : REGINA." The silver coinage consisted of half-crown, shilling, sixpence, groat, half-groat, and penny. The half-crown had for the type of its obverse the bust of Philip, below which was the date 1554, on the reverse the bust of the queen, a crown and date above. The type of the shilling is interesting, in that it is the only period of English coinage on which joint Sovereigns were represented face to face. This peculiarity gave rise to the humorous lines—

> "Still amorous, fond and billing,
> Like Philip and Mary on a shilling."

On the reverse is an oval shield of arms, over which is the denomination "XII." The remaining coins were of the usual types with abbreviated legends.

Elizabeth (1558–1603).

An attempt was made immediately after the accession of Elizabeth to bring the coinage of England into a better state by reducing the value of the base coins then current, and afterwards by producing a currency corresponding in weight and purity with its nominal value. The somewhat mixed coinage of gold may be distinguished as "standard" gold and "crown" gold. The standard gold consisted of sovereign or double-ryal, issued in 1558 to 1601, weighing 240 grains, the ryal and angel (see Fig. 160), half-angel and quarter-angel. The crown gold consisted of pound-sovereign, half-sovereign, crown, and half-crown. Milled coins were introduced between 1561 and 1572, the milled half-sovereigns weighing $87\frac{3}{11}$ grains, the current value being 6s. 8d. (see Fig. 159).

The silver coins of Elizabeth were of two distinct classes, hammered and milled. The first issue was

159

160

Fig. 159, Elizabeth, Milled Half-sovereign ; Fig. 160, Elizabeth Angel.

161

Fig. 161, James I Crown.

made by the old process of hammering and the later ones by the mill and screw, the chief feature of which was that it enabled the mint-masters to ornament the edges of the coins. Crowns and half-crowns were issued in 1601 and 1602. The chief coins in the hammered series were shilling, sixpence, groat, threepence, half-groat, three-half-pence, penny, three-farthings, and half-penny. The new milled money consisted of shilling, sixpence, groat, three-pence, half-groat, and three-farthings. As regarding types, the hammered money followed the lines of previous issues, on the obverse a crowned bust to left, the queen holding sceptre and orb. On the reverse a shield of arms on a cross with the usual emblems. The sixpences present a somewhat interesting variety, in that behind the head there is a rose, as is also seen on some of the smaller coins, notably the three-half-pence, and three-farthings. The silver half-penny is a little coin of 4 grains, the type of the obverse being a portcullis, on a reverse a cross moline with three pellets in each angle. The small coins of Elizabeth were the last bearing the name of the place of mintage. On some of the coins of Elizabeth are found the arms of Zealand, on others the letter "H" for Holland: these are said to have been so stamped for subsidies taken to the Low Countries. All the coins of Elizabeth were struck at the Tower Mint.

XII

THE STUARTS

CHAPTER XII

THE STUARTS

England and Scotland under one king—The current coins of Charles I —Obsidial money.

James I (1603–1625).

The accession of James to the throne of England made a considerable difference in the currency, in that in his person the Kingdom of Scotland was then joined to the throne of England; and, although at first there was little change in the Scottish currency, the foundation was laid for one uniform coinage of Great Britain, which followed in due course. James the First of England and Sixth of Scotland had had experience of a copper currency in the Northern Kingdom, and was, therefore, freed from the prejudice against the commoner metal which had been shown in such a marked degree by his predecessors on the English throne.

Of the gold of James I minted in England there were four issues, and on these coins the arms of Scotland and Ireland were quartered with the royal arms of England and France, on the same shield. The issue of 1603 was of crown gold. In 1604, however, the change in the title of the English Sovereign began, for on it James was described as "King of England, Scotland, France, and Ireland"; and in a later issue as "King of Great Britain." The Scottish coins of James's reign were distinguished by having the shield of Scotland in the *first* quarter of the arms. Some of the denominations of coins specially relating to earlier Scotch currency were retained (see Chapter XIX).

The gold of the second issue consisted of unite, double-crown, Briton-crown, thistle-crown, and half-thistle-crown. The third issue of rose-ryal, noble, angel, and half-angel; and the fourth issue of rose-ryal or thirty-shilling piece, spur-ryal or fifteen-shilling piece, angel, laurel, half-laurel, and quarter-laurel. Fig. 162 is a splendid example of a rose-ryal or thirty-shilling piece of the issue 1619–1625; on the obverse the king is seated on a throne, at his feet a portcullis. The shield is upon a cross fleury, within beaded circles; between them, in each of the quarters formed by the cross, are lis, rose, and lion.

The silver coins of James, for England, were of two issues only, with but slight differences in design. The first issue of 1603 consisted of crown, half-crown, shilling, sixpence, half-groat, penny, and half-penny. The second issue included the same denominations. In Fig. 161 is shown a very fine specimen of the crown of the second coinage; the legend on the obverse, on which the king is seated on horseback, reads: "IACOBVS . D . G . MAG . BRIT . FRAN . ET . HIB : REX." The shillings of the first issue have a similar device, the legend sur-

162

Fig. 162, James I Rose-ryal.

163

Fig. 163, Charles I "Declaration" Piece.

rounding the shield reading: "EXERGAT.DEVS. DISSIPENTVR.INIMICI" (*Let God arise; let His enemies be scattered*). The shillings and sixpences were of similar designs. The half-groat has on the obverse a rose, crowned, surrounding it, "I.D.G. ROSA SINE SPINA"; on the reverse a thistle, crowned, with the legend, "TVEATVR VNITA DEVS." Silver was scarce in James's reign, and that taken from the Welsh mines is distinguished by plumes of feathers as a mint mark. The other mint marks used during the reign of James I on silver and gold are of importance, in that they denote the year of issue, the coins not then being dated. They were as follows: 1603–4, thistle; 1604–5, fleur-de-lis; 1605–6, rose; 1606–7, shell; 1607–8, bunch of grapes; 1609, coronet and key; 1610, bell; 1611, mullet; 1612, castle; 1613, trefoil; 1615, cinquefoil and tun; 1616, book; 1617, crescent; 1618, cross; 1619, saltire and spur; 1620, rose; 1621–2, thistle; 1623, fleur-de-lis; and 1624, trefoil.

In the reign of James I a copper currency was commenced by the issue of what became known as "Harrington farthings." The patent to coin these little pieces, which only weighed 6 grains, was granted in 1613 to Lord Harrington of Exton. The type, which varies slightly, consists of crown and two sceptres on the obverse, and a harp on the reverse. Quite a number of mint marks are observable.

Charles I (1625–1649).

It has been stated that the coinage of Charles I was more extensive and varied than that of any of his predecessors. The regal issues of the ordinary currency were minted at the Tower Mint and also at several provincial mints. At the commencement of his reign Charles issued from the Tower unites, double-crowns, and British-crowns of crown gold; to these were added angels of the old standard gold. The silver consisted of crowns, half-crowns, shillings, sixpences, half-groats, pennies, and half-pennies. A little later from the provincial mints were issued three-pound pieces in gold, and ten-shilling and twenty-shilling pieces in silver.

In the first type, that of 1625–1626, the king, with few exceptions, is represented wearing the robes of the Order of the Garter. On the second type, 1626–1631, Charles is represented wearing ruff and armour, in the last regal issue the ruff being changed to a lace collar. Some changes in the form of the shield help the collector to arrange his pieces, the shield at first being square, afterwards oval. The larger coins represent the king on horseback, as shown in Fig. 164, which is a crown, the mint mark a harp. The usual legend on the obverse distinguishes the coins of Charles I from those of James I; and according to the customary change, Charles rides to left instead of to right. As on the coins of James, the legend on the reverse is "CHRISTO AVSPICE REGNO" (*Ruling under the guidance of Christ*).

Among the provincial mints of note were Aberystwith (mint mark, open book and crown); Bristol ("BR" and plume); Chester (three gerbs); Exeter (castle and rose); Oxford (plume and

164

Fig. 164, Charles I Crown.

165

166

Fig. 165, Charles I Carlisle Shilling ; Fig. 166, Charles II Pontefract Shilling.

"OX"); Shrewsbury (pellets and plumes); Weymouth (castle, helmet, and sometimes two lions); Worcester (pears); and York (lion passant and "EBOR"). The most notable legend used by Charles on the famous Oxford coins was that known as the Declaration type, on which was the legend, "RELIG. PROT. LEG. ANG. LIBER. PARL." This legend referred to the declaration Charles made at the time of the outbreak of the Civil War, which was that he would "Protect the Protestant Religion, Laws and Liberties of his Subjects, and Privileges of Parliament." (See Fig. 163.)

Then came the Civil War and the coinage of money of necessity. To some the most interesting pieces of English currency are those of irregular shape, which were minted with the authority of the king during the disastrous Civil War, during which Charles had frequently to flee from place to place, and during his stay in some of the baronial castles and strongholds had recourse to this method of providing himself with money to pay the troops, and for the requisite funds to maintain his cause. Some of these pieces were issued in his absence, but with his authority. For the most part they were dubbed "siege pieces," and from their quaint forms and designs, together with the peculiar circumstances under which they were issued, represent a curious break in British coinage.

The money of necessity during the unhappy struggle between Charles I and the Parliament, issued from for the most part temporary mints, was entirely of silver, and generally gave evidence of having been struck from pieces of plate given by generous supporters to their liege lord in his necessity. There are many odd and irregular values, the reasons for their issue having now been forgotten. Doubtless they then represented some recognized payment which necessitated that particular value of coin used under special conditions. These coins possess many similar characteristics, such as the gateway or towers of a castle, presumably intended to represent the besieged stronghold where they were minted. On many there is the abbreviated legend "OBS," which is of course short for *obsidio*, a siege. Among the rarest examples are those issued from Beeston Castle, a fortress which was dismantled by order of the Parliament on its surrender in 1645. These pieces are mostly oblong, and have a castle gateway for their type, in some instances twice struck, the value below it being in Roman numerals, above which are the denominational initials "S D." The twenty-four pence, or two-shilling piece, weighs 208 grains. There is a 1s. 4d. piece, weighing 130 grains, and several lower values. Carlisle Castle was besieged from 1644 to the end of the following year, during which period circular and octagonal siege pieces were issued of the values of three shillings, half-crown, and one shilling (see Fig. 165).

Colchester Castle surrendered in 1648, and apparently during the last months of the siege very interesting pieces of irregular shapes, some circular, and some oblong, were issued. The type was a five-towered castle, on it the abbreviated legend,

"Carolj fortuna resurgam" (*The fortunes of Charles shall rise again*).

Perhaps the most frequently met with siege pieces are those of lozenge shape, issued in Newark, on the obverse. The central design is a crown, with the royal initials "C.R." on either side. The denomination of the piece illustrated is "XXX." (thirty pence). On the reverse is the legend, "OBS. NEWARK. 1645." It will be remembered that Newark surrendered to the Scottish Army on May 8, 1646. There are many siege pieces of Pontefract, which castle was besieged by Cromwell himself. The siege of Pontefract is noteworthy in that its defenders did not surrender to the Parliament after the execution of Charles I. The defenders continued under royal authority to issue siege pieces; many of those issued towards the end of 1648 bore the name of Charles II, whom they then recognized as their lawful king. The Pontefract twenty-shilling piece is unique. There are, however, many shilling and two-shilling pieces, the legend adopted for these being "DVM. SPIRO. SPERO." (*Whilst I live, I hope*). (See Fig. 166).

Another group are those struck at Scarborough, in 1645. They cannot be mistaken, for in addition to the castle gateway on the obverse there is the legend of the reverse, "OBS. SCARBOROVGH."

There is an octagonal shilling of Pontefract issued after the death of Charles, bearing the legend, "POST MORTEM PATRIS PRO FILIO" (*After the death of the father for the son*). This appears to have been struck in 1648.

There were no copper coins minted in the reign of

Charles I other than the farthings or "Harrington" tokens as issued in the reign of James I.

Figs. 167 and 168 are coins from the Exeter Mint, the former a shilling dated 1645 and the latter a half-crown, dated 1644.

167

168

Figs. 167 and 168, Charles I Exeter Shilling and Half-crown.

169

Fig. 169, Commonwealth Twenty-shilling Piece.

XIII

THE COMMONWEALTH, AND AFTER THE RESTORATION

CHAPTER XIII

THE COMMONWEALTH, AND AFTER THE RESTORATION

Coins without the royal name, title, or arms—The Lord Protector issues coins with his portrait—Regal currency restored—The famous Petition crown.

The Commonwealth (1649–1660).

On the death of Charles, the Parliament recognized that it was important that they should issue without delay a new currency from which royal titles, and all emblems of the monarchy, were eliminated. That accounts, probably, for the marked contrast which the coins issued during the rule of the Protector present to those of any other period in English history. No doubt the new coins had an influence upon the people, who in using them would be reminded that the monarchy was abolished, and that the "Commonwealth of England" had taken its place. The legend or descriptive title of the issuers served for nearly all the pieces both in silver and gold. In the centre of the coins was the cross of St. George, on a plain shield, on the obverse; the reverse being occupied by the St. George's cross and the Irish harp.

The gold coins of the Commonwealth consisted of a twenty-shilling piece, a ten-shilling piece, and a five-shilling piece, the first-named weighing 140½ grains. The legend on these coins, which were sometimes called broads and half-broads, was "GOD WITH VS," the value being expressed in Roman numerals (see Fig. 169). The silver coinage was practically of the same type. The shield on the obverse, as will be noticed on referring to the illustration, is surrounded by wreaths consisting of branches of palm and olive; the silver coins consisting of crown, half-crown, shilling, sixpence, half-groat, penny, and half-penny, the last-named coin being without the wreath.

It is doubtful whether the coins of Oliver Cromwell were ever in regular use. If they were the circulation was small and very local. Most of the pieces which are obtainable are in good condition, all, however, are rare. They are easily distinguished by the bust of the Lord Protector, and the legend which reads, "OLIVAR. D.G. RP. ANG. SCO. HIB. & PRO." On the reverse is a shield of arms, in the upper left-hand quarter St. George's cross, also charged on the bottom right-hand corner of the shield. In the right-hand upper quarter is the cross of St. Andrew, and in the lower left-hand the Irish harp. In the centre of the shield is a small escutcheon on which is a lion rampant, the arms or crest of the Protector. Above the shield is a crown, the legend around being, "PAX QVÆRITVR BELLO" (*Peace is sought by war*). These coins are mostly dated 1656 and 1658. The gold coins consisted of a fifty-shilling

170 171 170

Figs. 170 and 171, Coins of Oliver Cromwell.

172

Fig. 172, Oliver Cromwell Crown.

piece, a broad or twenty-shilling piece, and a half-broad.

Oliver Cromwell, who was the first to letter the edges of coins, inscribed the edge of his rare fifty-shilling piece of gold, "PROTECTOR . LITERIS . LITERÆ. NVMMIS . CORONA . ET . SALVS" (*A protection to the letters : a garland and safeguard to the coinage*). The inscription on Cromwell's forty-shilling piece of silver was, "NEMO . ME . IMPVNE . LACESSET." (*No one shall hurt me with impunity*). In addition to this large coin there were crowns, half-crowns, florins, shillings, and pieces of nine-pence and six-pence. Of the crowns there are three varieties, those of Simon, Tanner, and a Dutch piece. The illustrations given in Figs. 170, 171, and 172 are taken from finely preserved specimens of these rare pieces. Fig. 170 is a two-shilling piece, a pattern by Tanner, of the same type as the nine-pence shown in Fig. 171 and the crown represented in Fig. 172.

Oliver Cromwell appears to have made a decided attempt to institute a satisfactory copper currency, although the coins he issued were never put into circulation, and are more correctly described as "pattern farthings" (see Chapter XVI).

Charles II (1660–1685).

On the Restoration a new currency became necessary without delay. An effort was made to place it on a better basis, and owing to the employment of other die-sinkers, Thomas Simon prepared his notable crown piece which makes the coinage of Charles II so noteworthy in the eyes of collectors.

An exceptional specimen of this piece, dated 1663, which has found a place in several noted collections, is illustrated in Fig. 173. Below the bust can be read distinctly in script *Simon*. On the reverse are the crowned shields of England, Scotland, Ireland, and France; in the centre the George within the Garter, on which is inscribed its motto, interlinked C's in each angle of the cross. The inscription twice circling the coin reads, "*THOMAS SIMON* MOST HVMBLY . PRAYS . YOVR *MAIESTY* TO COMPARE . THIS . TRYALL . PIECE . WITH . THE . DVTCH AND IF . MORE TRVLY . DRAWN . & EMBOSSD . MORE GRACE-FVLLY . ORDER'D . AND MORE . ACCVRATELY . EN-GRAVEN TO RELEIVE . HIM."

In the early years of Charles II both gold and silver hammered coins were struck in the old-fashioned way. The gold pieces consisted of the broad or twenty-shilling piece (see Fig. 174), the half-broad, and a crown, all made of "crown" gold, of the same fineness as the coinage of Charles I. Some were minted in 1660 without marks of value, those in 1661 having a numeral of value. The milled coins which were henceforth to supersede hammered money consisted of five-guinea, two-guinea, guinea, and half-guinea pieces. The five-guinea piece, weighing 647½ grains, may be taken as the type. On the obverse is a bust of the king, around it the legend, "CAROLVS II. DEI GRATIA." On the reverse four shields are arranged in the form of a cross with sceptres in the angles. The edge is inscribed "DECVS ET TVTAMEN" (*An ornament and a safeguard*), the object of the inscription being to prevent clipping.

173

174

175

Fig. 173. Simon's Petition Crown ; Fig. 174. Charles II Gold Broad (obverse) ; Fig. 175. William III Crown.

This legend, a quotation from Virgil, has been used on crown pieces in most of the mintages of the succeeding reigns, as well as on some of the larger gold coins. The two-guinea pieces were of similar design, but with milled edges. The guinea, which was destined to become a popular coin, was similar to the larger pieces. It took its name from the fact that most of the gold used at the mint at that time was imported by the African Company from Guinea. The mint mark to denote this special issue was an elephant, or an elephant and castle, under the king's bust.

The hammered silver was of three distinct issues, and consisted of half-crown, shilling, sixpence, groat, threepence, half-groat, and penny. The first issue was without numerals for value. The second had numerals but no inner circle. The third had both numerals and inner circle. The shield of arms was surrounded by the old motto, "CHRISTO AVSPICE REGNO," as on the coins of Charles I. The milled silver of currency consisted of crown, half-crown, shilling, sixpence, and Maundy fourpence, threepence, twopence, and penny. The crown had on the obverse a laureated bust of the king, and on the reverse two C's interlinked in each of the four shields which formed the cross, with the lettered edge as the five-guinea piece. The smaller coins were similar. Most of the silver used in this reign came from the West of England, and was distinguished by a rose, as mint mark, the silver from the Welsh mines being marked with a plume of feathers.

There are few collections of English silver without

some pieces of small denomination, mostly coins which were struck for the king's Maundy gifts, for even long after copper coins had been used for small purchases of currency, silver was thought the only fitting gift for the king to make in the fulfilment of the ancient custom annually observed at Westminster Abbey. Although not used in currency Maundy money is still minted in sufficient quantities to serve its historic purpose, and, incidentally, it provides collectors of small silver with sets of those much-valued coins. From the time when Maundy money was first struck up to the present time, with a few notable exceptions, all the four values have been issued annually. The gifts of doles on the Thursday before Good Friday were instituted as far back as the reign of Edward III and have been continuously given to the poor, the recipients being of the same number as the years of the life of the Sovereign. The established rule of quantity dates from 1563. In olden time the ceremony was performed by the Sovereign in person as an act of humility to commemorate the washing of the disciples' feet by our Saviour. This ceremony was observed until the reign of James II. The distribution of money at the present time is made by the Lord High Almoner and the Sub-Almoner, accompanied by Yeomen of the Guard. The Sergeant-Major of the Yeomen carries on his head a golden dish containing the Royal Maundy gifts, the gold in red purses, the silver in white. In recent years each man has received £2 5s. in lieu of the clothing monarchs of former days distributed, £1 10s. instead of provisions, and

£1 for the gold Maundy; the little bag of silver Maundy money in which collectors are chiefly interested totalling up to one penny for every year of the royal donor's age. After the ceremony the silver is generally exchanged for current coin of the realm, usually at a high premium, and so the Maundy sets pass in mint condition to collectors.

The specially coined currency dates from the reign of Charles II, by whom it was instituted in 1661, the first issue being groat, threepenny piece, half-groat, and penny. These coins were from dies by the celebrated Simon, and are the most recent specimens of hammered money. On the reverse is a shield of arms surrounded by the legend, "CHRISTO . AVSPICE REGNO." The second issue of Maundy in the reign of Charles II was milled; the values being designated by C's interlinked. For the copper currency of Charles II's reign, see Chapter XVI.

James II (1685–1688).

On the death of Charles II, his brother, the Duke of York, was proclaimed king, under the title of James II. His currency differs from the milled coins of 1670 only in the portrait and the inscription. His gold coins had an elephant and castle for their mint mark; some, however, were marked with an elephant only. These consisted of five-guinea, two-guinea, guinea, and half-guinea pieces. The five-guinea piece had the usual edge inscription, "DECVS ET TVTAMEN," the smaller pieces being milled. The silver consisted of crown, half-crown, shilling, sixpence, and a set of Maundy money, on the reverses of which were numerals, crowned.

The tin coins of this reign are referred to in Chapter XVI.

William and Mary (1688–1694).

After the abdication of James II, when William and Mary were firmly established on the throne, there was a new issue of all denominations, both in gold and silver, and the same weights and standards observed in the previous reigns of James II and Charles II were retained. The gold consisted of five-guinea, two-guinea, guinea, and half-guinea pieces, the type of the reverse is four shields cruciformly arranged, crowned, the arms of Nassau in the centre. The portraits of king and queen, laureated, distinguished the coinage of the joint reign from those minted when William reigned alone.

The silver currency of William and Mary consisted of crown, half-crown, shilling, sixpence, and a full set of Maundy coins. The crown piece is similar to that of William III alone, as illustrated in Fig. 175; it will be noticed that the four shields of arms are arranged in the form of a cross—England, Scotland, France, and Ireland; in the centre the arms of Nassau, as on the gold. In the angles of the cross, however, are "W M," the initial letters of the king and queen, in a monogram. There were three distinct half-crowns, the type of the first issue was the arms, on a square shield, crowned; the second, the arms, somewhat varied, were also on a square shield, on the first and fourth quarters the arms of France and England; but the third issue was of the same type as the then current crown. On the reverses of the Maundy coins were the numerals, crowned.

There were also tin and copper coins, for a description of which see Chapter XVI.

On the death of Mary, William reigned alone, and caused coins to be struck bearing his effigy. At that time the old hammered money which had been in circulation was recalled, and there was a very large recoinage of the metal, causing a loss to the country of nearly £3,000,000. To successfully accomplish the reminting of so many coins, within a short time, mints were again set up at Bristol, Chester, Exeter, Norwich, and York, supplementing the Tower Mint. The coins issued from the provincial mints are distinguishable by the "B" for Bristol, "C" for Chester, "E" for Exeter, "N" for Norwich, and "Y" for York.

There was an extensive issue of copper coins, fully described in Chapter XVI.

Anne (1702–1714).

There were several important issues of coins during the reign of Anne, divided into those before the Union with Scotland in 1707, and the joint currency issued afterwards. The difference chiefly consists in the arrangement of the shield of arms, the later issues after the Union having the arms of England and Scotland on the upper and lower shields, with France on the right and Ireland on the left. From that time henceforward the currency of Scotland became identical with that of England. For some time afterwards, however, silver continued to be struck at the Edinburgh Mint, the coins being distinguishable by the letter "E" under the bust. As already referred to, the word "Vigo" is found on gold and silver minted from the bullion taken from Spanish ships captured in Vigo Bay during Anne's reign. In addition to the gold, silver coins of the denominations of crown, half-crown, shilling, and sixpence were issued. There were also Maundy sets; but there is not, however, any penny of 1704, and neither penny nor fourpence of 1707.

The copper farthings of Queen Anne are referred to in Chapter XVI.

XIV

THE HOUSE OF HANOVER

CHAPTER XIV

THE HOUSE OF HANOVER

Additions to the royal titles—Many issues during the reign of George III—Rare gold pattern pieces.

George I (1714–1727).

No marked change was made in the currency of this country on the accession of George I, although there was a slight addition to the gold coins by the minting of a quarter-guinea in 1718.

The guineas of this reign, which were issued until 1727, were marked with an elephant and castle. The inscriptions on the coins of the Georges are somewhat puzzling in that the abbreviations of the legends upon them convey little or no meaning to present-day Englishmen. That on the obverse of the larger coins gives the king's title, in accord with the practice of previous Sovereigns, followed by "F.D." (Defender of the Faith), which had not been previously used on the currency, although the title had been bestowed by the Pope of Rome on Henry VIII, who used it on the Great Seal of England. On the reverse, however, were the king's German titles, "BRUN. ET. L. DUX. S. R. I. A. TH. ET. EL.," the English interpretation of which reads: "Duke of Brunswick and Luneburg, Arch-Treasurer of the Holy Roman Empire and Elector." On one of the left-hand side shields of arms will be noted the arms of the Electorate.

The chief distinguishing marks on the silver coins of George I are those denoting the source from which the metal used in currency was derived. Thus there are plumes for Wales, roses for the West of England, "SSC" for the South Sea Company, and two C's interlinked with plumes and "WCC" for the Welsh Copper Company. The complete denominations of this reign are: five-guinea, two-guinea, guinea, half-guinea, and quarter-guinea, in gold, and crown, half-crown, shilling, sixpence, and the Maundy set in silver.

George II (1727–1760).

George II struck coins in all the metals, the gold being minted in all the values employed in the previous reign, with the exception that no quarter-guineas were issued. The silver currency was the same also. On the gold coins the armorial bearings were emblazoned on one shield, but on the silver coins on separate shields in the form of a cross. Roses and plumes as mint marks are conspicuous on the silver. On the large pieces the quartering of the shields is well represented; in the centre instead of the arms of Nassau there is the Star of the Order of the Garter. On some of the gold coins there are the letters "E.I.C." under the king's bust, indicating that the pieces

Fig. 176, George II Five-guinea Piece; Fig. 177, George III Two-guinea Piece; Fig. 178, George III Half-guinea; Fig. 179, George III Five-guinea Piece.

were struck for the use of the East India Company; on others the name "LIMA," showing that they were made from bullion captured from the Spaniards; and on some coins an elephant under the bust. The piece illustrated in Fig. 176 is a five-guinea of 1731.

Collectors should note carefully the distinctive types of the two issues in all the currencies of George II. They are known respectively as "old" head, engraved by John Tanner, and "young" head, by John Croker.

The copper coins of this reign are referred to in Chapter XVI.

George III (1760–1820).

During the long reign of George III several important changes took place in the coinage in both the issues and denominations. Of gold there were four issues, the first consisting of guineas, half-guineas, and quarter-guineas; the second is distinguished as the issue of spade guineas and half-guineas, so called from the spade-shaped shield of arms, and by the seven-shilling pieces. The third issue was that of 1801 to 1813, the guinea issued in the last-named year being known as the Garter sovereign or guinea.

There was a change in the style and title of the king after the Act of Union 1800, when the king's title became (abbreviated on the coins) "Georgius Tertius, Dei Gratia, Britanniarum Rex, Fidei Defensor." The fourth and last issue of gold of George III was that of sovereigns and half-sovereigns, superseding the guineas. On the reverse was the well-known type of St. George and the Dragon. On the reverse of the half-sovereign, however, there was a shield of arms crowned, instead of the patron saint, within a garter.

There were three issues of silver coins; the first, which was made in 1763, consisted of shillings only, and they are somewhat scarce, for only a small quantity was issued. There was another issue of shillings and sixpences in 1787.

It was about that time that the Bank of England was empowered to issue Spanish dollars, countermarked with a small head of George III in an oval. Those dollars passed current for 5s. In 1804 a further supply was issued, stamped with an octagonal punch, and shortly afterwards some of the dollars were reminted as Bank of England tokens. The dollar or crown tokens were supplemented by pieces of the nominal values of three shillings and eighteenpence.

It was in 1816 that a very large issue of new silver took place, that issue consisting of crowns, half-crowns, shillings, and sixpences; and many of those pieces are still met with in circulation. The Maundy money of George III followed the type of the current issues, with the exception of the year 1792, when a distinct change was made, for that year only, in the type of the numeral of value, which took the form of script writing, and became known as "wire" money, from the delicate wire-like writing of the numeral. Maundy money of that year is the scarcest of any of the series. Arabic numerals were again used in the third issue, and in 1816 the type of bust of

George III as seen on his later coins, was used for royal Maundy gifts.

The illustrations relating to this reign are all gold, taken from exceptionally fine pieces. Fig. 179 is a five-guinea piece dated 1777; a variety in which the lovelock on the left shoulder is especially clear; on the reverse is an ornamental shield, crowned, with the usual arms and inscription. Fig. 177 represents a two-guinea piece, dated 1768; the reverse is similar to the larger coin, but a different obverse by Tanner. The half-guinea of 1775 is a beautiful pattern piece. The coin illustrated in Fig. 180 is a rare pattern crown, in silver, by W. Wyon, and is dated 1817; the head on the obverse being the laureated head used on the current coins of the later issue of George III; the reverse, a remarkable design, consisting of three female figures emblematical of the United Kingdom of England, Scotland, and Ireland, each having her national emblem at her feet; in the exergue there is a rudder and a palm branch.

For Colonial issues see Chapter XVII, and for copper currency see Chapter XVI.

George IV (1820–1830).

The coins of George IV are for the most part current at the present time. The gold currency included two issues; the first, 1821–1825, consisting of double sovereign, sovereign, and half-sovereign. With the exception of the obverse of the double sovereign, and the reverse of the half-sovereign, the dies used were the work of the famous die-sinker

Pistrucci. In the second issue, however, extending from 1825–1830, the dies were engraved by W. Wyon, who copied Chantrey's bust of the king, thereby obtaining a very flattering likeness.

There were three issues of silver; the first, 1820–1823, consisted of crown, half-crown, shilling, and sixpence. The second, 1823–1825, was slightly different in type, but of the same denominations. The third issue of 1825–1829 consisted of half-crown, shilling, and sixpence. Maundy money of all the values was issued.

The type of the reverse of the silver crown was St. George and the dragon, and that of the reverse of the first half-crown the arms on a garnished and crowned shield, the decorative emblems rose, shamrock, and thistle being added. On the reverse of the second issue the arms were placed on a plain shield crowned and circled by the Garter and the collar of the Order. On the third issue the arms were on a garnished shield, which was surmounted by a helmet. A notable feature was the "Lion" shilling, on the reverse of which was a lion standing upon a crown—the crest of the Sovereign. A sixpence was also issued in lesser quantities, such pieces being now much scarcer and more valuable than the shilling, especially when in mint condition.

For copper and Colonial currency, see Chapters XVI and XVII.

William IV (1830–1837).

There is no special feature of interest in the coinage of William IV, the inscription on whose coins reads in the Latin form, "GULIELMUS," with the exception perhaps, of the restoration of the groat. The gold consisted of sovereign and half-sovereign, the type of the reverse in both instances being a shield of arms crowned. The silver consisted of half-crown, shilling, sixpence, groat, and the Maundy fourpence, threepence, twopence, and penny. The Maundy fourpence must not be confused with the groat of currency, on the reverse of which was the figure of Britannia, with the inscribed denomination "FOUR PENCE" above. On the reverse of the half-crown of William IV was a shield of arms on a royal mantle, crowned. On the reverse of the shilling was the value, "ONE SHILLING," in the centre of a wreath; and on the reverse of the sixpence "SIX PENCE" within a wreath.

For copper regal and Colonial coins, see Chapters XVI and XVII.

XV

VICTORIA,
EDWARD VII,
AND
GEORGE V

CHAPTER XV

VICTORIA, EDWARD VII, AND GEORGE V

Patterns, and pieces withdrawn—Commemorative currency—Money in circulation to-day.

Victoria (1837–1901).

The coinage of Queen Victoria brings the collector in touch with still current coins of the realm ; the chief interest, however, lies in the pattern pieces which form a distinct group of numismatics. In Fig. 181 a beautiful five-pound pattern piece by W. Wyon, R.A., is illustrated. The type of the reverse is the queen, as Una, guiding the British lion. There are, however, some features of interest to note in Victorian coins, some few of which are already almost entirely withdrawn from circulation. The denominations of the gold coins of Victoria were five-pound, two-pound, sovereign, and half-sovereign pieces. In the early portion of the queen's reign the sovereign and half-sovereign alone represented the gold of currency. On these were the queen's head, and titles on the obverse and surrounding the shield of arms on the reverse. In the second issue the type adopted for the reverse of the sovereign was that of St. George and the dragon. The most notable coins of the reign were the Jubilee issue, put into circulation in June, 1887, when Queen Victoria celebrated the fiftieth year of her reign. Very many five-pound and two-pound pieces were struck, and for a short time quite a number of the latter circulated, but they were gradually withdrawn by collectors and by others who retained them as souvenirs.

The type of the larger gold coins was the queen's head with arched crown and veil; on the reverse St. George and the dragon. The two-pound piece, sovereign, and half-sovereign, were similar. There was a second issue of the Jubilee type in 1893, when a notable addition was made to the queen's title, declaring her to be Empress of India as well as Queen of Great Britain and Ireland.

The first issue of silver, in 1838, consisted of crown, half-crown, florin, shilling, sixpence, groat, and threepence, to which must be added the Maundy silver, distinguishable from the then current groat and threepence by the use of the numeral, crowned, the Jubilee bust of the Queen being adopted for the Maundy money in 1888. The chief coin of note in the silver currency was the very beautiful Gothic crown, circulated only in small quantities, and regarded to some extent as a pattern piece, although apparently many were struck. It was of the type which afterwards became so familiar in the Gothic florin of currency. The first two-shilling piece struck in 1849 was smaller in size than the one with which most people to-day are acquainted. On account of

180

181

Fig. 180, George III Pattern Crown ; Fig. 181, Victoria Pattern Five-pound Piece.

the omission of the letters "D.G." (Dei Gratia) it became known as the "Godless" florin, and was soon displaced by the Gothic florin of 1851, a type which continued to circulate until quite recent days.

The type of the crown of currency of the first issue showed the youthful head of Victoria on the obverse, and on the reverse a shield of arms, the edge being inscribed with the old motto, "DECVS ET TVTAMEN." The second issue was of the Jubilee design. The coins of that issue were supplemented by the introduction of the four-shilling piece or double florin, slightly smaller than the crown piece, the reverse being not unlike that of the Gothic crown. It is technically described as obverse, bust to left with arched crown and veil; reverse, four shields crosswise, cantoned with four sceptres. The coin was never popular, and has almost passed out of use although still current. The florin of the last issue had upon it in clear type the legend, "TWO SHILLINGS, ONE FLORIN." On the reverse were the shields of Scotland and England above, that of Ireland below, behind two sceptres, and in the field the rose, shamrock, and thistle. The shilling had upon its reverse, "ONE SHILLING" with a wreath, above it a crown. The type of the second issue of 1887 was a shield surmounted by an arched crown, round it the badge of the Garter. The type of the third issue was three shields, all crowned and enclosed within a Garter, in the field a rose, a shamrock, and a thistle. The groat, or fourpence, was not coined after 1856, and was withdrawn from currency some years later.

Edward VII (1901–1910).

The currency of gold and silver minted during the reign of his late Majesty King Edward VII is familiar to all. In the first issue, following the usual custom, gold of the higher values was struck; but although made current coin of the realm, neither two- nor five-pound pieces were circulated.

The type of the silver differed but very slightly from that of the later coins of Queen Victoria. The denominations, too, were the same, with the exception that no double florin was issued. The chief difference between the coins of Edward VII and those of Queen Victoria, is that of the change of title to "BRITANNIARVM OMNIVM REX" (King of *all* the Britons). The type of the florin was that of Britannia standing on a ship; and of the shilling, the royal crest, which is a lion on a crown.

In order that collectors may understand how to designate their current silver correctly, the following extracts from the Proclamation determining the designs of the new coins in the reign of Edward VII is given: "Crown:—the inscription shall read: 'EDWARDVS VII. DEI GRA: BRITT: OMN: REX: FID: DEF: IND: IMP.', and on the reverse shall be the image of St. George, sitting on horseback attacking a dragon with a sword, with a broken spear upon the ground. There shall be the date of the year, and on the edge of the piece the raised letters DECVS ET TVTAMEN. On the reverse of the half-crowns shall be the ensigns armorial of the United Kingdom, contained in a shield, surmounted by the Royal Crown, and surrounded by the Garter, on which shall be the motto, HONI SOIT QUI MAL Y PENSE, with the inscription, 'FID: DEF: IND: IMP:' On the reverse of the florin shall be the figure of Britannia, standing upon the prow of a vessel, her right hand grasping a trident, and her left resting on a shield. Every shilling shall have the same obverse, impression, and inscription as the half-crown, and on the reverse the Royal crest, the lion on a crown. Every sixpence shall have in the centre of the piece the words SIX PENCE, with an olive branch on the one side and an oak branch on the other, surmounted by an oak crown. The Maundy silver, a fourpence, three-pence, two-pence, and penny, shall represent the King's effigy, his inscription, and the value of the coins in figures surmounted by a Royal crown. The edge of the Maundy money shall be plain, not milled."

George V

The gold and silver coins of his present Majesty George V, whose style is "King of Great Britain and Ireland, and the Dominions beyond the Seas, Defender of the Faith, and Emperor of India," were ordered by Royal Proclamation, made at the Court of St. James. The Proclamation contained a description of the coins for circulation in this country, fixing their denominations on the lines of the previous reign. Of these there is nothing special to relate, as coins in mint preservation of all the values can be taken out of circulation at any time they are required to fill up a cabinet of modern coins, but specimen sets as supplied by the Mint, in cases, are the most favoured as having the mint bloom upon them, and every other detail perfect. The chief innovations of recent issues of coins of his Majesty, are those associated with the Colonial currency, more particularly referred to in Chapter XVII.

XVI

REGAL COPPER COINS

CHAPTER XVI

REGAL COPPER COINS

Early patterns for copper coins—Half-pennies of tin and copper with metal plugs inserted—Many issues and a new denomination in the reign of George III.

As it has already been indicated, an attempt was made to introduce a copper currency in the reign of Queen Elizabeth, but the earlier coins must be regarded more as experimental and as pattern pieces than as coins struck for general circulation. At that time, when Elizabeth minted her pattern penny in copper, there was strong prejudice against the base metals, for the country was then flooded with inferior continental coins and tokens, abbey pieces and the like of various types. The inscription on the pattern referred to reads, "THE PLEDGE OF A PENNY," stamping it at once as being more of a token than a current coin.

In the reign of James I the noted Harrington farthings were issued by patent granted in 1613, the type being a crown over two sceptres, in saltire, the legend or title reading, "IACO . D . G . MAG . BRI :" On the reverse was a harp, crowned. Of these coins there are many varieties, and numerous mint marks are collectable. These little pieces were very thin and irregularly struck, making them easily counterfeited.

On the accession of Charles I, the farthings were proclaimed lawful currency, and a fresh patent was granted for seventeen years to the Dowager Duchess of Richmond and Sir Francis Crane with right to coin them. The inscription was then altered to, "CARO : D . G . MAG : BRIT." Of these there are many variations in the abbreviations of the royal titles, and in the mint marks used. There is a variety frequently met with, showing a rose, crowned, on both obverse and reverse.

After the Civil War pattern pieces were issued from the mint; but none of the copper coins of either the Commonwealth or of the Lord Protector Cromwell can be regarded as current money—certainly not "regal."

On the Restoration, Charles II made a determined effort to supply much-needed coins of the lower denominations in copper, but it was not until 1672 that the regal half-pennies and farthings of currency were circulated. That issue marked a decided change, in that instead of the very small Harrington coins, the half-penny and farthings by Royal Proclamation made regal tender for sums of less than sixpence were of large size and weight. It was on those—half-pennies and farthings—that the figure of Britannia, so like the type of Britannia on the Roman coins of Hadrian and Antoninus Pius, was first adopted as the type of our English copper currency. A curious difference is made in the draping of the figure of Britannia on the two coins; in that on the farthing Britannia is represented with one leg undraped, both being covered on the half-penny. The legend on the obverse reads, "CAROLVS . A . CAROLO," the king's bust being in Roman armour, and his head laureated. The legend on the reverse, surrounding the figure of Britannia, is "BRITANNIA." The designs of both half-pennies and farthings are the same.

The current English coins of James II were of tin with a square plug of copper in the centre; on them the legend reads, "IACOBVS SECVNDVS." The farthings and half-pennies were identical in type, the figure of Britannia appearing on the reverse in each case.

The first issue of coins in the baser metal in the joint reign of William and Mary, was of tin, with a square plug of copper, as in the preceding reign. The busts of the king and queen were side by side, William wearing armour, the queen a mantle. The legend around both half-penny and farthing was "GVLIELMVS . ET . MARIA," the edge of the half-penny being inscribed "NVMMORVM . FAMVLVS." The same difference between the half-penny and farthing as in previous reigns is noticeable in the issues of William and Mary, in that on the farthing Britannia is represented with one leg bare. In 1694 copper half-pennies and farthings were struck from similar dies to those used for the tin coinage, but there was no legend on the edge.

After the death of Mary copper half-pennies and farthings were issued of similar design to those of the previous reign, the legend around the king's bust which was in Roman armour, with head laureated, being "GVLIELMVS TERTIVS." The farthings were similar, the date, however, was placed after the legend "BRITANNIA," and not in the exergue as on the half-penny.

The reign of Queen Anne is notable in that there

were no extensive issues of copper. A number of pattern farthings were struck, however, the reverse in the centre of the three shown in group 182, being considered to be the design selected for the intended current coins, which were not issued in any quantity; the other two reverses were patterns only.

Three years after George I came to the throne halfpennies and farthings were struck. On the obverse was the king's bust, with short hair, laureated, and in armour, within a circle of very broad graining, with the edge plain. These coins date from 1717 to 1724 inclusive.

There were two distinct coinages of regal copper in the reign of George II. The first, commonly known as "young" head, was ordered in the absence of the king in Germany. The types of both halfpennies and farthings were identical. In 1740 there was an issue from new dies, known to collectors as "old" head, the dates occurring from 1740 to 1754.

During the long reign of George III there were several distinct departures in the copper currency of this country. The first issue of copper from new dies was, however, not made until 1770, ten years after the king came to the throne. These were similar to those of the previous reigns, the king, however, looking to right, the legend being altered to "GEORGIVS III. REX." Farthings of that issue were identical in design. In 1797 coins were issued from the Soho Mint, in Birmingham. The legend was in sunk letters on a flat rim; on the reverse it was "BRITANNIA," and the date "1797." The emblematical figure of Britannia is seated on a rock; by her side waves, and a three-mast ship in the distance. Britannia holds an

182

Fig. 182, Anne Pattern Farthings.

183

184

Fig. 183, George III Half-ackey (obv.) ; Fig. 184, George III Barbadoes Penny.

olive branch in her right hand, in her left a trident, and beneath the shield is the word "SOHO." The denominations were two-penny, penny, half-penny, and farthing. The farthing, however, was a pattern piece.

The next issue of copper took place in 1799, and consisted of half-pennies and farthings struck from new dies. In 1806 there was another issue of copper, consisting of penny, half-penny, and farthing.

The first issue of copper in the reign of George IV consisted of farthings only. The design did not please the king, and a new one was engraved a few years later, from which pennies, half-pennies, and farthings were struck. That design represented a bust of the king, laureated, but without any drapery. On the reverse was the figure of Britannia without the olive branch, and without the lion which had been introduced into the first design of farthings, which had been struck during this reign. In the exergue were intertwined the rose, shamrock, and thistle.

In the reign of William IV the type of the previous reign was retained in the design of the reverse. In fine preservation copper coins of William IV are rather scarce.

The copper coins issued in the early years of the reign of Queen Victoria were from dies engraved by William Wyon. The three denominations were repeated as in former reigns, supplemented by half-farthings and one-third-farthings. These small pieces, however, never seem to have been popular in this country, but they were used in Malta. Quarter-farthings were also struck in limited quantities, chiefly for use in the Colonies. In 1860 the copper currency of this country ceased, and a new coinage of bronze was substituted. The bronze as at present used consists of 95 parts of copper, 4 of tin, and 1 of zinc, the issue in bronze metal being penny, half-penny, and farthing, and one-third-farthing for Malta. The design was quite different to the copper. The queen, somewhat older-looking, was represented laureated, and with drapery, embroidered with a spray of roses, shamrocks, and thistle, on her shoulder. On the reverse Britannia was once more restored to the possession of the waves and the three-masted vessel, to which was added a lighthouse. The designs of the three values were identical. It is interesting to note that the weights of the smaller coins, the half-penny and farthing, were more in proportion than that of the penny. The copper coins of 1886, onward, present the draped head of the queen wearing a coronet, ribbon, and the Order of the Garter, to her titles being added that of "Empress of India."

The bronze coins of King Edward VII were issued by the authority of a Proclamation which came into force on the first day of January, 1902. The legend read: "EDWARDVS VII. DEI GRA. BRITT : OMN : REX ; FID : DEF : IND : IMP :" On the reverse Britannia is seated on a rock surrounded by the sea, in her right hand a shield which rests against the rock, in her left hand a trident, the same design for all three denominations.

The bronze coins of King George V are similar in design, and are very familiar to all loyal subjects of his Gracious Majesty the King residing in Great Britain or Ireland.

XVII

BRITISH COLONIAL CURRENCY

CHAPTER XVII

BRITISH COLONIAL CURRENCY

The collection of early issues—Curious West Indian money—The East Indian series extended over a wide range—Some interesting European islands currency.

THE currency of British Dominions beyond the Seas has grown so extensively during recent years, owing to the rapid increase in the trade and commerce of the Colonies, and the development of the Empire of India, that it is impossible in one short chapter to fully describe the coins of currency in the possessions of his Majesty King George the Fifth. The coins referred to, therefore, are for the most part those which have long been obsolete, and for which collectors have to seek among the curios of coinage, and not in the tills of traders.

To simplify the classification of Colonial coins it will be convenient to divide them into the following groups: "African," "Australian," "Asiatic," "West Indian," and "European." (The coins of former British possessions in North America, and those of Canada, are described in Chapter XVIII.) For many years the greater number of coins current in

British Colonies were strictly speaking tokens, and in describing those which may for convenience' sake be classified as regal coins of currency, there will be some little overlapping.

Africa.

The African dominions of Great Britain have not only been extended during recent years, but they have been peopled with Europeans, many of whom are now engaged in local trade and commerce, as well as in inter-Empire trading; consequently the very limited currency which once sufficed for the native African peoples who traded under the protection of the British flag would now be totally inadequate to the needs of those vast countries in Africa which now belong to Great Britain.

At one time the African Company trading with the West Coast issued moneys suitable for the people with whom they traded. Their coins for the most part took the names of native money and weights, and in some instances their forms. The African Company, towards the close of the eighteenth century, circulated silver coins, the denominations of which were ackey, half-ackey, quarter-ackey, and eighth-ackey. On the obverse was the cipher of George III, "G.R." with a crown, and the date, 1796. On the reverse the legend accompanying the shield of the Company with supporters and crest was: "FREE TRADE TO AFRICA BY ACT OF PARLIAMENT, 1750." A fine pattern half-ackey of 1818 is given in Fig. 183.

The West African Colonies include vast tracts of country, the latest addition to the moneys of West

Fig. 185, Madras, Double-pice ; Fig. 186, Bombay, Pattern Mohur ; Fig. 187, Ceylon ; Fig. 188, Bombay, Half-anna ; Fig. 189, Pattern Rupee.

Africa being silver coins, issued in 1913, of the nominal values of two shillings, one shilling, sixpence, and threepence. Their dimensions, weights, and fineness are the same as the corresponding coins of the United Kingdom. On the obverse is a portrait of King George V, and on the reverse of the higher values an oil-tree palm, with the legend, "BRITISH WEST AFRICA."

The early coins struck by the Sierra Leone Company, in 1791, show upon their reverses a lion preparing to spring, beneath it the simple legend, "AFRICA." The denominations of these coins in silver were dollar, 50, 20, and 10 cents; and in copper, penny and cent.

The token currency of the Cape of Good Hope and of Natal, struck about the middle of the nineteenth century, includes a few rare pieces in silver as well as copper. The most notable piece is a Griqua Town half-penny in copper; there are also five-penny and ten-penny pieces in silver, the type of the latter being a dove bearing an olive branch.

The currency of the Transvaal, issued during the presidency of President Kruger, is of comparatively recent date. Those issues, bearing his portrait bust, are obtainable in fine preservation, in several denominations, and although used when the country was a Republic, may now with propriety be included in a collection of British African coins. The Transvaal and the Orange River Colony now use coins bearing the effigy of George, King of all the Britons and of British Dominions beyond the Seas.

Australia.

The Commonwealth of Australia has now an independent coinage of its own; upon the silver is the Australian arms and the motto, "ADVANCE AUSTRALIA." For a long time past gold has been coined at the Sydney and Perth Mints. The earlier pieces of interest to a collector, however, are chiefly tokens, as for many years, indeed until the third quarter in the nineteenth century, Australian traders issued their own tokens for local circulation. In South Australia, in 1862, a gold coin was issued by the Government, but no silver or copper coins other than the tokens referred to are to be found among the old coins of Australia.

Asia.

The varied issues of coins for the different countries and states in Asia ruled over by the Emperor of India include not only native pieces, but independent issues, before the Government undertook to provide an adequate currency in values and denominations suitable for the people. The East India Company for many years planted the British flag, and maintained the commercial relations between Great Britain and India. It did its best to supplement the native and other moneys in use, and in some instances was able to substitute its issues for the coins of other nations then trading in the Far East.

The East India Company was founded in 1600. At that time Spanish dollars had an almost worldwide circulation, and were much employed in India. This did not suit the purposes of the Sovereign of these realms, and it is said that Queen Elizabeth deemed it necessary that Asiatics should understand and realize that besides the King of Spain there was a monarch who ruled in her far-away island home. She authorized the issue of coins of the values of crown, half-crown, shilling, and sixpence, which were to be used concurrently with Indian rupees of native mintage; and she prohibited the East India Company from importing or using Spanish dollars in India. On these coins of Elizabeth the portcullis, crowned, and the Royal Arms of England figured. It will be remembered that the portcullis or cross-barred gate referred in English silver coins of the Tudor period (see Chapter XI) was the badge of the Beauforts, who were descended from John of Gaunt. They took their name from the *beau fort*, or beautiful castle, in France, and henceforward used the portcullis of the castle gate as their badge. The crown of the East India Company's issue of that period was small and thick, measuring about 1¼ in., weighing, however, 425 grains. On the reverse was the legend, "O.POSVI.DEVM.ADIVTOREM.MEVM" (*I have made God my helper*).

In the reign of Charles II a mint was established at Bombay, and the coins of the values of rupee, half-rupee, fanam, and half-fanam in silver, and the pice and its multiples in copper, were issued. Rupees were struck at Bombay in the reign of James II. A change was made in the next issue of coins for India struck at Bombay in the time of George II, which appear to have been of copper or lead; their values were double pice, one pice, and half-pice. On the obverse was a crown, with "G.R." above it and "BOMB." under it; on the reverse the Company's bale mark. There were some additions to the currency of India in the reign of George III, several of them being purely Oriental in type, among them a very curious two-kapang piece issued by the East India Company in 1787. Collectors usually group the coins of the Bombay Presidency together, and keep a keen look out for the rupees of seventeenth-century dates. Many of the copper pice are scarce; there are also some few lead pieces. The gold mohurs of the Bombay Mint are fine early pieces. The one illustrated in Fig. 186 is a pattern mohur, the type of the obverse a lion under a palm-tree, on the reverse the name of the place and the date 1828. Fig. 188 is also a pattern from the Bombay Mint; it is a half-anna and is dated 1821.

The coins of the Bombay Presidency include mohurs from the Calcutta Mint. The collectable varieties of silver rupees are also numerous. In the Presidency there were at one time several important mints, including those at Murshidabad, Patna, Benares, and Ferrukabad; the values of the coins issued being mostly described in Bengali, Persian, and Nagri characters.

Coins of the denominations of double pagoda and pagoda were struck at Madras, the type being an Indian pagoda surrounded by stars, and on the reverse the figure of Vishnu. The silver coins issued about the same time were half-pagoda, quarter-pagoda, and fanam. Small coins, in copper, of the divisional values of the rupee, were also struck

Fig. 190, Shanghai, 2 Mace ; Fig. 191, Pattern Mohur ; Fig. 192, Pattern Two Mohurs ; Fig. 193, Hong-Kong Dollar.

at Madras. A twenty-cash piece was issued in 1804; on its obverse were the Company's arms and supporters, and on the reverse the value and the date in, Arabic numerals. Fig. 185 is a double pice, on a thick dump, struck in Madras.

At various times efforts have been made to secure greater uniformity in the currency, and quite a number of patterns have been struck. In Fig. 192 a fine pattern double mohur struck in 1854 is shown; on the obverse is the head of Queen Victoria, on the reverse a lion under a palm-tree, above which is the legend, "EAST INDIA COMPANY." Fig. 191 is a pattern mohur of 1870, not unlike the issue of the then current mohurs. A pattern rupee of William IV, dated 1834, is shown in Fig. 189; on the obverse the legend "WILLIAM IIII, KING"; on the reverse is a lotus flower over the denomination of value.

During recent years many coins of modern types have been issued for India from the Royal Mint. Those circulating in the reign of Queen Victoria were supplemented in the time of Edward VII by a further issue of other denominations; and still more recently coins bearing the effigy and titles of his present Majesty King George V, have been put into circulation throughout the presidencies and native States constituting the Indian Empire. In this connection it may be well to note that nickel has been employed to supplement the usual metals of currency, notably by the issue of a one-anna piece; but it is said that the older pieces issued in 1835, when the coinage of India was made uniform, are preferred by the natives, and are still extensively used.

There are a number of coins which were formerly used in Ceylon; among them native money and coins known as double rix dollars, supplemented in 1815 by rix dollar pieces. The copper series include the divisional parts of the dollar. In 1827, and again in 1870, half- and quarter-farthings were minted in England for use in Ceylon; and in later years five-cent, one-cent, half-cent, and quarter-cent pieces have been minted. In 1892 a nickel coinage consisting of fifty, twenty-five, and ten cents was issued. Fig. 187 represents a 96 stiver piece in silver—a curious and interesting old coin.

The island of Sumatra was early one of the possessions of the East India Company. In 1783 a two-sookoo piece in silver was issued there, bearing in Malay characters the legend *Money of the Company*, 2 *Sookoos*, and on the reverse "FORT MARLBORO." Copper coins were struck in 1804, the legend reading, "EAST INDIA COMPANY," to which was added the value.

There are silver rupees of Penang, dating from 1788, on the reverse the legend, "PRINCE OF WALES ISLAND"; and several pattern pieces in silver and copper.

Before the British possessions now known as Straits Settlements had become such an important area special coins similar to the cent in use in the Straits Settlements were struck for use in British Honduras. On the obverse was the head of Queen Victoria, adorned with a coronet, and the legend

"VICTORIA QUEEN." On the reverse, "BRITISH HONDURAS, ONE CENT."

The earliest coins issued in British Guiana were made out of old Spanish dollars, pieces and fragments being countermarked. An extensive coinage, however, was issued in 1809 consisting of silver two-guilder, one-guilder, half-guilder, and quarter-guilder pieces. Although these coins were marked on the reverse, "TOKEN," they were issued by Government authority.

Many very beautiful pattern pieces intended for Hong Kong have been designed. One of these—a pattern dollar—dated 1864, is illustrated in Fig. 193; on the obverse is a small bust of Queen Victoria with the simple legend, "VICTORIA QUEEN," on the reverse four shields with Chinese characters forming a cross, oak and laurel leaves in the angles the legend, ONE DOLLAR," and the date "1864." The collectable current issues are dollars, half-dollars, fifty, twenty, ten, and five cents. There are also scarce pattern cents in copper. Fig. 190 illustrates a pattern two-mace piece, dated 1867, intended for use in Shanghai.

West Indies.

Spanish dollars have circulated freely in the West Indies, and the early attempts to introduce British currency there do not seem to have been very successful. Among the patterns which have been struck, that illustrated in Fig. 209 is of special beauty The obverse was of the same type as the penny struck, by George IV for use in Ireland. The reverse legend, "COLONIAL," suggests that the intention was to make it an acceptable piece throughout many of our Colonial possessions.

In Barbadoes a penny was struck in 1788, the type of the obverse being the bust of a negro, wearing a plume of three ostrich feathers, below, the legend, "I SERVE"; on the reverse a pineapple. In 1791 there was another issue, consisting of penny and half-penny, the type of the reverses being as illustrated in Fig. 184, the central design was the king seated in a marine car. In Bermuda or Sommers Island coins of the respective values of shilling, sixpence, threepence, and twopence, in base metal, were issued in 1616; the type on the obverse was a wild boar, the money being afterwards known as "hog" money. A copper penny was struck in 1793, on the obverse the bust of George III, on the reverse a man-of-war in full sail. In more recent years tokens and other pieces which indiscriminately circulated in the West Indies have been replaced by coins prepared at the Imperial Mint.

In the year 1891, by an Order in Council, four-penny pieces coined at the British Mint were made current as legal tender in British Guiana, Grenada, St. Vincent, St. Lucia, Trinidad, and Tobago. Towards the end of the year 1908 the issue of 5-cent and $\frac{1}{4}$-cent copper coins for Ceylon, was superseded, the 5-cent piece having been found inconvenient and clumsy, a nickel bronze coin of 60 grains weight was introduced, its type similar to the new Indian one-anna piece; but to prevent confusion the coin was made square, with rounded corners. On the one side was a portrait of King Edward, with the legend "KING AND EMPEROR," and on the other a numeral, denoting its value, the value being repeated on either side of the numeral in Sinhalese and Tamil characters.

Europe.

The Channel Islands have for a century or more possessed a separate copper currency. In Guernsey the copper coins, changed to bronze in 1861, consist of eight, four, two, and one double pieces. On the obverses are the arms of Guernsey, on the reverses the values and date. In the reign of Queen Victoria there were several separate coinages of copper and bronze in Jersey. The first, which was in 1841, consisted of one-thirteenth, one twenty-sixth, and one fifty-second part of a shilling in copper. The second coinage in 1866, in bronze, was of the two higher denominations; the third coinage of 1877 marked a change in the denomination, which became one twelfth, one twenty-fourth, and one forty-eighth of a shilling. The Jersey piece illustrated in Fig. 196 is an exceptionally fine penny token of 1813; on the obverse the head of George III and "JERSEY"; on the reverse the figure of Commerce seated and the legend, "ONE PENNY TOKEN."

Separate coins have always been circulated in Gibraltar. The first issue of copper, which was made in 1842, consisted of two-quart, one-quart, and half-quart. On the obverse was the bust of Victoria, and on the reverse a castle with a key under it, above it "GIBRALTAR."

The chief coin struck for use in Malta is the one-third farthing, first issued in 1827 in copper. A further supply was issued in the reign of William IV in 1835, and again in 1844, in that of Queen Victoria. The bronze issues superseded copper in 1866.

When the Ionian Islands were under the protection of Great Britain (1815–1864) silver coins of the value of 30 oboli were issued, the type of the obverse being the winged lion of St. Mark, and that of the reverse Britannia seated. The copper coins were of the same types. An issue of bronze coins for use in Cyprus, consisting of piastre, half-piastre, and quarter-piastre, first made their appearance in 1878.

XVIII

IRELAND AND THE ISLE OF MAN

CHAPTER XVIII

IRELAND AND THE ISLE OF MAN

Ancient ring money—Coins of the Kings of Ireland—Separate issues under the English Sovereigns—"Gun" money—Manx copper.

SOME of the early coins of Ireland are interesting in that they represent a currency earlier than that known in any other part of the United Kingdom. These ancient moneys consisted of rings of gold, silver, and brass, which are said to have been graduated according to Troy weight in multiples of the pennyweight. The first coins of which there is any authentic record are those of the Kings of Dublin, who struck silver pennies not unlike early Saxon pieces, or those of the Kings of Scotland. The first of this series was that of Ifars I (870–872); followed by pennies of Anlaf IV (962–981), Sihtric III (989–1029), Anlaf V (1029–1034), Anlaf VI (1041–1050), and Ifars III (1050–1054). Those of the last named are typical. On the obverse is the king's head with radiated crown, and an inscription which means "King Ifars of the Northmen of Dublin"; on the reverse is a cross, in the angles of which are ornaments.

The Kings of Waterford issued pennies, the most notable being those of Regnald II (1023–1036).

Æthelred II and Canute of England are said to have struck coins from the Dublin Mint. The first authentic coins issued by the Kings of England as lords or kings of Ireland, however, were those struck by John—some being minted before his accession to the English throne, in virtue of his title, "Lord of Ireland." They bear mint marks of Dublin and Waterford, some few later ones being struck at Limerick. Henry III issued pennies and half-pennies from Dublin in 1248, and Edward I and Edward III issued pennies, half-pennies, and farthings in silver from Cork, Dublin, and Waterford, the names of the mint towns being traceable on them. The type of the coins struck in Ireland by those kings and their predecessors was that of a full-faced bust within a triangle.

The next coins of any note were those struck in Dublin in the reign of Henry VI. The first issue, of 1425, consisted of pennies only, and were of the same type as the English money; the second issue of 1460 consisted of groat and penny. A copper half-farthing was struck for use in Ireland in 1460. All these coins are distinguishable from those used in England by the name of the mint town.

In the reign of Edward IV coins in silver, copper, and brass were minted from the Dublin and other Irish mints. The first issue of that reign was in 1461, and it consisted of groat and penny; the second, in 1463, also of groat and penny; and the

195

196

197

198

Fig. 195, Isle of Man Pattern Half-penny ; Fig. 196, Jersey Penny
Figs. 197 and 198, Isle of Man Pattern Pennies.

third, in 1465, was similar. The fourth coinage in 1467 was issued from mints at Carlingford, Dublin, Galway, Limerick, Trim, and Waterford, and consisted of groat, half-groat, penny, half-penny, and farthing. There was a seventh coinage in 1478, notable for the type of the reverse, which was three crowns, the arms of Ireland from the reign of Richard II to that of Henry VIII. A billon farthing, also one of copper, were issued in Dublin in 1462. Silver groats and pennies were issued in the reign of Richard III.

A number of the coins of Henry VIII bear the Dublin mint mark, and in that reign additions were made by the coinage of other denominations of sixpence, threepence, three-half-pence, and three-farthings. The types of some of these pieces were a shield of arms on the obverse, and a harp, crowned, on the reverse.

Mary, reigning alone, struck silver coins for Ireland of the denominations of shilling, groat, half-groat, and penny. Dated coins of the reign of Philip and Mary were issued in 1555.

Elizabeth struck coins for Ireland in silver and copper. The first issue in 1558 consisted of shilling and groat, coined out of base money recalled from circulation in England, while in 1561 similar coins of good silver were issued. These coins may be distinguished from English moneys of contemporary dates by the crowned harp on the reverse. In the reign of James II no special change was made in the coins, which continued to be issued from similar dies to those used by Elizabeth. It was in this reign that the Harrington farthings were struck for use in Ireland as well as in England.

The only regal money struck for Ireland during the reign of Charles I consisted of farthings in copper. This currency, however, was supplemented by the "money of necessity" struck during the Civil War.

This section of Irish coinage is extremely interesting to advanced collectors. The most important are the crown, half-crown, shilling, and smaller pieces known as Inchiquin money, so called after Lord Inchiquin, Vice-President of Munster, who was an active operator against the rebels in the South of Ireland. The crown weighed 464 grains, the smaller pieces being for the most part irregular in weight as well as in shape. The Ormonde money took its name from the Marquis of Ormonde, who was Viceroy of Ireland in 1643, when he received a warrant from Charles I to create money of necessity. The chief denominations of that issue and their weights are: crown, 456 grains; half-crown, 228 grains; one shilling, 90 grains; sixpence, 45 grains; fourpence, 30 grains; threepence, 22 grains; and twopence, 15 grains. The type was an irregular oval. On the obverse were the letters "C.R.," within two circles, beneath a crown; on the reverse, within a double circle, was the value in Roman numerals. Irregularly shaped coins were struck in Dublin and in a few other places. There are some half-crowns, commonly called "Blacksmiths' money," because of the very rough workmanship. They, too, were issued under an order from Charles I, which stated "That it is directed that the plate of this Kingdom be coined with the ordinary stamp used in the moneys now current." On the obverse was an effigy of Charles I on horseback, in his right hand a sword resting on his shoulder. There is a plume on the horse's head, the trappings being ornamented with a broad cross. It has been pointed out that the horse apparently stands without any ground on which his hoofs may rest. The legend around reads, "CAROLVS. D.G. MAG. BRIT. FRA. ET. HIB. REX."

In the year 1642 Kilkenny money of similar characteristics to other money of necessity was issued. The chief emblems and types were a castle, the letter "K," and two crossed sceptres behind a crown. The Kilkenny money consisted of half-pence and farthings in copper, forming a distinct variant from the silver pieces struck from old plate.

In the reign of Charles II the St. Patrick half-pennies and farthings were struck. These are curious little pieces, the obverse having for its type King David kneeling and playing a harp. On the reverse is the figure of St. Patrick with a crozier in his left hand and a shamrock in his right. He carries a shield on which are three castles, the arms of Dublin, the legend of the reverse being "ECCE GREX" (*Behold the Flock*). On the farthings (see Fig. 199) the legend, which varies, reads, "QVIESCAT PLEBS" (*May the people remain in quietude*). The peculiarity of the design of the farthing is that of St. Patrick, who, standing near a church, is shown stretching his hand over a number of reptiles, which are hurrying away. It is said that the reptiles typified the rebels!

After the Restoration some farthings were issued in Ireland under authority of a patent granted to Sir Thomas Armstrong. In the reign of James II copper half-pennies were issued between 1685 and 1688. Then came the money of necessity struck after James's abdication of the English throne, mostly of mixed metal known as "Gun" money, including a half-crown and lesser denominations. Groats were struck of white metal in 1689. There were also pewter and brass half-pennies. The only coins struck in Ireland during the reign of William and Mary were half-pennies, the type of the reverse being a harp, crowned. Half-pennies were also struck when William reigned alone.

The silver coins issued in Ireland during the Georgian period by the Bank of Ireland were tokens and not regal currency. Some of the copper coins, however, although technically tokens were, like the Harrington farthings of the reigns of James I and Charles I, issued in Ireland as well as in England, semi-regal, in that they were issued under patent from the Crown. The most important issue was that of William Wood, who, under patent granted in 1722, coined copper half-pence and farthings. The patent rights had been granted to the Duchess of Kendal, who sold her concession to Wood, described as an ironmonger, of Phœnix Street, Seven Dials, for £10,000. The issue was limited to 360 tons, a pound of copper being minted into half-pence and farthings of the total value of half-crown. Wood's half-penny is inscribed, "GEORGIVS DEI GRATIA REX," around a laureated bust of the King, on the reverse the legend "HIBERNIA," in the centre the figure of Hibernia, seated, holding a harp; in her right hand a palm branch.

In the reign of George II there were two issues of half-pennies and farthings. George III's first copper coin for Ireland was a half-penny, issued in 1766; the inscription "GEORGIVS III. REX," surrounded the laureated head of the King, the type of the reverse being a harp, crowned. There were farthings also. There was a second issue of both values in 1805, struck at the Soho Mint.

In the reign of George IV there were special regal copper coins—pennies and half-pennies—for Ireland, dated 1822 and 1823; but since the latter year there has been no special issue for Ireland, the currency of Great Britain being used.

The Isle of Man.

The Isle of Man, in the midst of the Irish Channel, is so closely allied to this country that we wonder how it was that it was allowed to remain a private possession so long. It was held under the Crown of England by Sir John de Stanley, as early as the year 1406, and remained in possession of the descendants of the Stanleys, the Earls of Derby, (with the exception of a short period during the Commonwealth) until it was acquired by the British Government in 1765 from the Duke of Athol, into whose hands it had come by heirship There are coins of the island dating from 1758. On them the ducal coronet and famous triune—the three legs, booted and spurred—emblem of three in one. The first collectable coin of the series is the penny of 1709; in the centre of the field of which is the crest of the Stanleys, the eagle and child above the cap of maintenance, over it the motto "SANS CHANGER" (*Without changing*). The well-known legend which always surrounds the triune, in which it will be noticed the feet always point to the left, is "QUOCUNQUE GESSERIS STABIT" (*Wherever you will cast it, it will stand*).

In the reign of George III regal pennies and half-pennies in copper were struck for use in the island. On the obverse was the king's head laureated; on the reverse the triune, and the motto. No regal money was issued for the Isle of Man during the reigns of George IV and William IV. The last coins for separate use in the island were issued in 1839, in the reign of Queen Victoria. That issue consisted of penny, half-penny, and farthing. In 1840, by Act of Parliament, the coinage of Great Britain superseded the Manx coins then current, and became henceforth the only money of currency in the Isle of Man.

The accompanying illustrations represent scarce pattern pieces; Fig. 195 is a pattern half-penny dated 1721, and is struck in brass; Fig. 197 and Fig. 198 are pattern pennies.

XIX

COINS OF SCOTLAND

CHAPTER XIX

COINS OF SCOTLAND

Early silver pennies—A fine series of gold—The coins of Mary Queen of Scots—Scotch coins under the kings of Great Britain.

THE first coins of the Kingdom of Scotland of which we have any record, are those of David I, who, in 1124, issued pennies from mints at Berwick, Carlisle, Edinburgh (see Figs. 201 and 202), and Roxburgh. Henry, Prince of Scotland, created by Stephen of England Earl of Northumberland, struck pennies at Bamborough and Corbridge (see Figs. 200 and 204). Malcolm IV and William the Lion also issued pennies, a rare piece of the latter being shown in Fig. 205. In the reign of Alexander II (1214–1249), many pennies were struck at Berwick and Roxburgh, mostly crude in design. There were several issues during the reign of Alexander III, who set up mints at Aberdeen, Berwick, Glasgow, Lanark, and Perth. John Baliol struck pennies and half-pennies; one of his coins, of the long cross type, is a half-penny, in two of the angles of the cross being stars. Alexander was followed by Robert Bruce, who issued pennies, half-pennies, and farthings without the names of any mint towns upon them.

David II was the first Scottish king who struck gold. His nobles were of similar types to those of Edward III of England. His silver coins consisted of groat, half-groat, penny, half-penny, and farthing. Robert II struck silver coins of all the denominations, chiefly at Dundee, Edinburgh, and Perth. Robert III issued gold coins called "St. Andrews," on the obverse of which are the arms of Scotland, crowned, on the reverse a representation of St. Andrew with arms outstretched, on either side a *lis*. His billon coins, which were current as pennies and half-pennies, were struck at Aberdeen, Edinburgh, and Inverness.

On the demy, a beautiful gold piece of James I, is a lion rampant in the centre of a lozenge-shaped shield; on the reverse St. Andrew's Cross, in the corners of which are fleurs-de-lis. The silver coins of this reign were groats, struck at Edinburgh, Linlithgow, Perth, and Stirling. Coins of James II are met with in the three metals, gold, silver, and billon. Coins of James III are also met with in gold, silver, and billon, and a few in copper. A typical silver penny has on its obverse the king's head with a legend round it, and on the reverse a long cross with three pellets in the angles, and the name of the mint town, "VILLA EDNBVRGH" (Edinburgh).

Coins were struck in the reigns of James IV and James V. During the reign of Mary some new denominations were issued. There were six issues of gold: the first, in 1543, consisting of abbey crown; the second of a twenty-shilling piece; the third, in 1553, of lions and half-lions; the fourth of ryal and

Fig. 199, Charles II St. Patrick Farthing; Fig. 200, Henry, Prince of Scotland, Penny; Figs. 201 and 202, David I Pennies; Fig. 203, Mary, Queen of Scots, Gold Ryal; Fig. 204, Henry, Prince of Scotland, Penny; Fig. 205, William the Lion, Penny.

half-ryal; the fifth of a ducat; and the sixth of a crown: a three-pound piece is shown in Fig. 203. The silver coins may be divided into the coins of Mary before her marriage with Francis; those struck during her married life; the coins of her widowhood; those after her marriage with Darnley; and lastly those issued from the death of Darnley to the dethronement of Mary. The hardhead of Mary, on the obverse of which is "M," crowned, and on the reverse a lion, is a fairly common piece. There is also a nonsunt of billon, on which is the monogram of Mary and Francis.

During the reign of James VI the two chief divisions of currency were those struck before his accession to the English throne, in 1603, and those struck afterwards.

The coins of the first period include gold, silver, billon, and copper. There were seven issues of gold: the first, in 1575, consisting of a twenty-pound piece; the second, in 1580, of a ducat or noble; the third, in 1584, of a lion noble, two-thirds lion noble, and one-third lion noble; the fourth issue in 1588, a thistle noble; the fifth issue, in 1591, a hat piece; the sixth issue, in 1593, a rider and half-rider; and the seventh issue in 1601, of a sword and sceptre and a half-sword and sceptre.

The silver coinage of James VI consisted of eight issues. The first issue in 1567, sword dollar or thirty-shilling piece, two-thirds sword dollar, and one-third sword dollar; the second, in 1572, noble or half-merk; the third, in 1578, double merk, and merk; the fourth, in 1581, sixteen-shilling piece, eighteen-shilling piece, four-shilling piece, and two-shilling piece; fifth issue, 1582, forty-shilling piece, thirty-shilling, twenty-shilling, and ten-shilling pieces; the sixth, in 1591, balance half-merk and balance quarter-merk; the seventh, in 1593, ten-shilling, five-shilling, thirty-pence, and twelve-pence pieces; and the eighth issue, in 1601, thistle merk, half-thistle merk, quarter-thistle merk, and eighth-thistle merk.

Of billon coins there were four issues: the first, in 1583, plack and half-plack; the second issue, in 1588, hardhead; the third, hardhead and half-hardhead; and the fourth, plack only. With the last issue terminated the billon coins of Scotland.

On the accession of James VI to the throne of England there was a change in the currency of the two kingdoms, and in 1604 an order was made to secure uniformity in type, quality, and weight. Gold coins were issued in 1605 and again in 1610, both issues consisting of unite, double crown, half-crown, and thistle-crown. Silver coins were issued the same year, the denominations being sixty shillings, thirty shillings, twelve shillings, six shillings, two shillings, one shilling, and half-shilling. To understand these curious and apparently large value coins, it is necessary to remember that Scotch values in gold and silver as compared with English money were in the proportion of twelve to one. Thus a twenty-shilling piece English was equivalent to £12 Scotch, and the English shillings to twelve shillings Scotch.

The copper coins of James VI after his accession to the throne of England consisted of turner or twopence, and half-turner or penny. On the turner the king's title is given as "KING OF GREAT BRITAIN, FRANCE, AND IRELAND"; on the obverse a three-headed thistle, and on the reverse a lion rampant, crowned.

The Scotch coinage of Charles I was similar to the later issues of the preceding reign. Several new coins in silver were introduced, but the current values remained in the proportion of twelve to one. The first issue of Scotch coins, in 1625, consisted of unite, half-unite, and quarter-unite. The second issue was the same, with the exception of the addition of an eighth-unite. The first issue of silver took place in 1625, and it consisted of three pounds (Scottish), thirty shillings, twelve shillings, six shillings, two shillings, shilling, and half-shilling; the last-named piece being equal to the English half-penny. Up to that time Scotch coins were *all* hammered, but the fourth issue of Charles II was made by the mill and screw, and it consisted of sixty shillings, thirty shillings, twelve shillings, six shillings, half-merk, forty-pence and twenty-pence pieces. The fifth issue, in 1642, consisted of three-shilling and two-shilling pieces. The copper coins of that period were turners and half-turners.

During the Commonwealth no separate coins were struck for use in Scotland. After the Restoration, however, Charles II issued silver and copper coins. There were two separate issues, the first in 1664, consisting of four merks, two merks, merk, and half-merk, all dated. In the second issue, in 1675, the denominations were dollar, half-dollar, quarter-dollar, eighth-dollar, and sixteenth-dollar. The copper coins were turner, bawbee, and bodle, the two last being new coins. The bawbee, which is very common, has for the type of the reverse a thistle, crowned. The type of the bodle is a sword and sceptre under the crown, on the obverse; a thistle on the reverse.

In the reign of James II of England coins of the Scotch values of forty shillings and ten shillings were issued. On the obverse of these coins was the king's bust, laureate, under it the numerals of value, a distinguishing mark which helps to locate the silver of James struck for Scotland. No copper was issued in this reign.

William and Mary struck silver coins for separate use in Scotland, but no gold. The silver consisted of sixty shillings, forty shillings, twenty shillings, and five shillings, and the copper of bawbees and bodles. After the death of Mary, William continued to strike coins for use in Scotland, adding two gold coins, a pistole, and a half-pistole. The type of these, the last gold coins of the Scottish series, was remarkable; under the king's bust was the sun rising out of the sea—a design adopted because the gold was supplied by the Darien Company, and was brought over to this country in a ship named the *Rising Sun*.

Anne struck coins in silver for Scotland, there being two issues, one before the Union and one after. The values of the first were ten shillings and five shillings, and the last issue, 1707, crown, half-crown, shilling, and sixpence, of the same types as English money of the period, the only difference being the letter "E" under the bust, denoting that they were minted in Edinburgh. With that issue the separate regal money for the Kingdom of Scotland was brought to an end.

Thus closes the story of the regal coins of Great Britain and Ireland, and the countries included in the British Empire. Collectors following the outline given, and noting the chief distinguishing marks outlined should not have much difficulty in deciphering their specimens and fixing their dates approximately.

XX

AMERICAN COINAGE

CHAPTER XX

AMERICAN COINAGE

The currency of other nations—British moneys—After the Declaration of Independence—South American issues.

THE collector goes back to the utmost limits of the history of the civilization of any country in the coins of which he specializes. In many instances he is able to touch the borderland of mythology. Indeed, in the coins of the earlier nations there was a close relationship between their treasuries and their temples. That explains to some extent the frequent pictures of emblems of the old gods of fable and romantic history. The American Indians, however, had no coins, and although they had religious faiths none of them are reflected on the subsequent issues from the American Mint. The coins which have passed current in North America at different periods have, it is true, been varied in metal, and in the monetary standards adopted, but Liberty and Independence are depicted rather than old traditions.

In collecting the coins of the New World the earliest examples met with are those which originated with the countries of those adventurers and sailors by whom the great continents of North and South America were discovered, and made known to the Western World. Thus we find that the coinage of those vast areas dates only from the sixteenth century; although perhaps a few still earlier coins were seen and handled by the natives of America, extracted, perhaps, from the pockets of Columbus and his followers. Spanish, Portuguese, and English colonies were in turn planted in many different parts of the two continents, and the coins employed by early traders were those of the respective countries with which they traded.

Spanish dollars were early used in South America, and the developments from the types of those early pieces and their divisions found favour in North America as well as in the Southern States. The greatest interest, however, centres in the coins of the North American possessions of Great Britain, and in those of the vast territories which eventually became independent and formed the federation known as the United States, which from the time of the Declaration of Independence had an independent currency. The first issues of the coins of the United States are not ancient as collectors understand the term, but they are obsolete and many of them exceedingly rare and valuable.

The coins of Maryland, and Massachusetts—or New England—form the basis of a cabinet of North American coins. For many years Spanish dollars were freely circulated, but gradually English silver attained a greater hold in trading circles; but as none of the coins used by North American traders

Fig. 206, Massachusetts, Oak-tree Shilling ; Fig. 207, Massachusetts, Pine-tree Sixpence ; Fig. 208, Maryland, Sixpence ; Fig. 209, West Indian Dollar.

at that time had any distinctive marks it did not form any specific currency. In the seventeenth century Maryland was a part of Virginia; but by Charter dated June 20, 1632, the Province, which afterwards became separate, was granted to Lord Baltimore, who was descended from an old Flemish family named Calvert. He sailed up the Potomac to an island he named St. Clement. Arriving among friendly natives he took possession of the land, and gave the place in which he settled the name of St. Mary. Maryland as a place-name has been associated with that event, but it is said the true naming was after Henrietta Maria, the Queen of Charles I.

The coinage of Lord Baltimore is that which forms the first pieces in a cabinet of North American coins. It consisted of shillings, sixpences, and groats in silver; but alas! it was short-lived, for the English Government ordered the seizure of the dies from which the coins were struck under the supervision of Lord Baltimore himself, a few months after they had been issued. On the obverse of these scarce pieces, which are dated 1659, is the bust of Lord Baltimore, surrounded by the legend, "CAECILIVS: DNS:TERRAE-MARIAE"; on the reverse is, "CRESCITE: RT: MVLTIPLICAMANI:" with the arms of Lord Baltimore under a crown, the mark of value "XII" at the side. Smaller pieces are similar, but they are marked "VI"; one of these is illustrated in Fig. 208. There is also a penny believed to have been a pattern and never circulated.

Another early issue of American coins is found in

those pieces which were issued by the General Court of Massachusetts, in 1670. They were minted in Boston, the die at first being simply "N.E." for New England, on the obverse; the numerals of value denoting shilling, sixpence, and threepence on the reverse. An improvement in type was made a little later by the addition of an outer ring, and the values and the name of the place of circulation—"MASSACHUSETTS"—on the obverse, and "NEW ENGLAND" on the reverse; a fine "oak-tree" shilling is illustrated in Fig. 206, and a "pine-tree" sixpence in Fig. 207, thus showing both varieties. On the copper piece already referred to there is an elephant on the obverse, and on the reverse the pious legend "GOD PRESERVE NEW ENGLAND, 1694." Coins similar to those struck in New England were issued for use in Carolina, the country granted to Lord Clarendon and others in 1660. The inscription on those pieces reads, "GOD PRESERVE CAROLINA : AND THE : LORDS PROPRIETERS."

The "Plantation" pewter half-pennies of James II were struck specially for use in Virginia. The most important series for that country, however, were those of copper or brass, struck in 1773. They bore a striking resemblance to the gold guineas then being issued in England, and might well have been mistaken for those numerous counters which were struck a few years later, modelled on the guinea then circulating. On these pieces, around the laureated bust of George III on the obverse, is, "GEORGIUS III. REX"; on the reverse a shield of arms and date, together with the legend, "VIRGINIA." A somewhat curious inscription is seen on a token at that time circulating in Connecticut, which reads on the reverse, "I : AM : GOOD : COPPER : VALVE ME AS YOU PLEASE : ."

THE DOMINION OF CANADA

The vast country we call Canada has been the scene of rapid development and commercial activity during the last few decades. In the early days of its upbuilding, however, the story of its progress tells of gradually bringing under cultivation vast areas, now wheat-fields, and in the more northern parts of the extension of trade with those whose lives were spent amidst the wilds of forests, and lands where wild animals still roamed and held sway. The trade of the Hudson's Bay Company was carried on by barter and seldom in coin. There came a time, however, when money and not kind was needed. The issue of an adequate coinage was very slow, and the various coins which chiefly constituted the currency were very mixed, being for the most part somewhat of a token currency, although most of the issues were "by authority." The local banks began to assume a position in trade of the country, and assisted traders by the issue of tokens; many of these interesting pieces are now scarce, especially in mint preservation, a condition so important in copper tokens, the beauty of which lies largely in their fine condition, rubbed specimens being of quite small value in comparison.

In considering the money which circulated in the early days in Canada, the first calling for mention is that very fine series of so-called Rosa-Americana coins issued in 1722, in the reign of George I. These pieces, which were of mixed metal or alloy, known as "Bath Metal," consisted of the values or denominations of two-penny, penny, and half-penny. They were struck by William Wood, who had obtained a patent of fourteen years' duration. The destiny of the issue was defined in the order for their mintage, described as: "For the King's Dominions and Territories in Canada." The first issue, which consisted of the mintage of about three tons of metal, took place in 1722; on these pieces the king's title ran: "GEORGIUS: D: G: MAG: BRI: FRA: ET: HIB: REX," the reverse was chiefly occupied with a rose, uncrowned, the legend above it reading: "ROSA AMERICANA," to which was added "VTILE. DVLCI" on a label. In the reign of George II, in 1723, a two-penny piece of similar design was issued. The one illustrated in Fig. 210 is a pattern two-pence dated 1724—an exceedingly rare variety.

More than a century elapsed before the issue of traders' and bank tokens, already alluded to, took place. It seems almost inconceivable that the Government should have allowed this immense country to make shift with tokens and almost any piece of metal enterprising men chose to put into circulation. Some of these pieces were little more than traders' advertisements, and did not even pretend to serve the purposes of trade. Such pieces, although some of them are scarce, do not appear worthy of inclusion in a coin collector's cabinet, and are, therefore, omitted in the following review of the

Fig. 210, Rosa-Americana, Two-pence ; Fig. 211, Newfoundland, Two Dollar ; Fig. 212, Nova Scotia, Half-cent ; Fig. 213, Nova Scotia, One cent ; Fig. 214, Montreal Bank Token.

tokens which served the honest purposes of trade, and in many instances had a long circulation, and no doubt helped storekeepers to provide the much-needed change.

Montreal was one of the most go-ahead towns, and it is there that we find the supply most prolific. The first piece bearing date, calling for special mention, is the Wellington half-penny, of 1816; on the obverse is the head of Wellington with the legend, "HALFPENNY TOKEN 1816," within a beaded circle; on the reverse a ship and the place-name "MONTREAL." A so-called "Commerce" token was issued in Montreal, by Francis Mullens & Son; and others by T. S. Brown & Co., and R. Sharpley. The North-West Company's token, of 1820, is a very rare piece; on the obverse is the bust of George III, and on the reverse a beaver—a curious feature of this token being that it is always met with holed.

The Bank of Montreal issued many tokens, the dies being very varied. They may be distinguished by the legend, "AGRICULTURE & COMMERCE BAS CANADA," or "BANQUE DU PEUPLE MONTREAL." The one illustrated in Fig. 214 is a remarkably fine specimen, dated 1839; on it is a view of the Bank, with legend, on the obverse the usual motto, "CONCORDIA SALUS," around the emblems on a Garter, on the ribbon, incuse, is the inscription, "BANQUE DU PEUPLE MONTREAL."

The Quebec Bank issued pennies in 1827, and again in 1852; on these latter the legend reads, "PROVINCE DU CANADA. DEUX SOUS." The type is very interesting, the figure of Commerce pointing to a ship on the River St. Lawrence, other attributes being a beehive, fruit, cereals, and a beaver, together with a view of the citadel of Quebec. The Bank of Montreal tokens of 1837 show a view of the front of the Bank, a half-penny of the same date having as a curious device on the obverse a native of the country wearing a Phrygian cap, the legend being "PROVINCE DU CANADA"; on the reverse are the arms of the city within a Garter, on which is inscribed "CONCORDIA SALUS."

The Province of Ontario offers collectors a somewhat earlier variety in a half-penny token of the Copper Company of Upper Canada, of 1794; the type of the reverse is a river-god reclining against an urn, from which water flows; the legend reading, "FERTILITATEM DIVITIUS QUE CIRCUM FERREMUS."

The Bank of Upper Canada issued what is known as "George and Dragon" half-pennies, in 1850, the initials "R.H. & CO." stand for Ralph Heaton & Co., by whom they were minted.

With the change of 1876 and the issue of cents, the copper currency of the Dominion was put on a proper basis, and what may be termed the modern coinage of Canada established. The cent of the first year of issue has upon the obverse the diademed bust of Queen Victoria within a dotted circle, the legend reading, "VICTORIA DEI GRATIA REGINA CANADA" within a dentated border; on the reverse is "ONE CENT 1876" within a dotted circle, surrounded by a wavy line, to which are attached sixteen maple leaves. Of these pieces there are proofs in nickel, copper, and bronze.

PROVINCE OF NOVA SCOTIA.

Under the name of Acadia, Frenchmen founded a colony, afterwards known as Nova Scotia, now merged into the Dominion of Canada. Previous to the year 1832, token pieces were the only separate issues for that colony. One of these tokens is of special interest, recording as it does an important historic event; on the obverse is the bust of Commander Broke, the legend reading, "BROKE, HALIFAX . NOVA SCOTIA"; on the reverse are ships which are intended to represent the *Shannon* and *Chesapeake*. It will be remembered that in the famous fight between the two vessels Broke commanded the *Shannon*.

From the year 1832 there was a desultory issue of copper coins for use in Nova Scotia. They consisted of pennies and half-pennies, those of the first issue having upon the obverse the laureated head of George IV, the type of the reverse being a large thistle, and the legend, "ONE PENNY TOKEN." There was a change in the type of 1856, on the obverse being the diademed bust of Queen Victoria, on the reverse branches of hawthorn leaves and May-flowers; the half-pennies of these several issues being similar in design to the concurrent issues of pennies. There was a change in the currency in 1861, and the issues of coins, and of stamps, too, were denominated in cents instead of pence. On the obverse of the 1861 issue the queen was represented wearing a robe, on the shoulder of which was embroidered a rose, a shamrock, and a thistle; on the reverse there was a circle of trefoils surmounted by a crown, above it the value: "ONE CENT." A very beautiful and rare pattern cent, of 1861, is illustrated in Fig. 213; it differs from the variety issued for general circulation in that the lettering is larger, and the crown is encircled by a heavy wreath of roses and leaves.

In 1871 there was an issue of regal money for use in Prince Edward Island, which had been named after Edward, Duke of Kent, the father of Queen Victoria. There was only one denomination—a cent, in bronze. The type of the reverse was unusual, consisting of a group of three maple-trees, typical of the three divisions of the island, under the shadow of a large spreading oak, typifying the protective Mother Country. The regal coins for use in Newfoundland, first issued in 1860, were based on the dollar standard. There was a two-dollar piece in gold; half-dollar, twenty-cents, ten-cents, and five-cents in silver; one-cent in bronze. On the obverse of all these coins there is the head of Queen Victoria, and on the reverse the legend "NEWFOUNDLAND." The coin shown in Fig. 211 is a pattern two-dollar piece struck in bronze; it is dated 1864, and is rare if not unique in type.

THE UNITED STATES.

The Declaration of Independence in 1776 abolished all irregular coinage in the States, which then became united in one federation. A scheme of finance was soon promulgated, and the Government of the United States founded its system on the dollar, which was authorized April 2, 1792, the Independence having been acknowledged by Great Britain in 1783.

The coinage of the thirteen States of the Union consisted of gold and silver, shortly afterwards supplemented by the issue of copper cents, some of the earlier patterns and even current types of which are now rare.

The type of the gold of 1792 was the head of Liberty, wearing the Phrygian cap, the legend "LIBERTY" being flanked by thirteen stars, the number of original States; on the reverse was the eagle with a laurel wreath in its beak, around it the legend "UNITED STATES OF AMERICA," the values of that issue of gold were eagle, half-eagle, and quarter-eagle. There was a change in the type of the reverse in 1796, when the stripes were emblazoned for the first time on the shield borne by the eagle.

In 1834 there was a distinct change in the type, a profile bust being substituted for the head of Liberty, which had hitherto been generally used; around the head was the descriptive legend "LIBERTY" on a band across her brow, but she had lost her cap. A one-dollar piece was introduced in 1849; later in the same year a gold double eagle was added. In February, 1853, a three-dollar gold piece was minted, but in 1900 both the three-dollar and one-dollar pieces were discontinued.

The year 1873 brought a change in the standard of currency in the United States, when the gold dollar of 25·8 grains and $\frac{9}{10}$ fine was made the unit of value instead of the silver dollar, which had hitherto been the standard.

The silver dollar, first issued in 1792, had for its

type the draped head of Liberty, differing somewhat from the type of the head used on the gold currency. The figure of Liberty on the obverse was accompanied with stars and legend; on the reverse there was the eagle with outstretched wings, surrounded by wreaths. The denominations of that first issue were dollar, quarter-dollar, dime, and half-dime. The type of the dime was changed in 1837, and the piece was discontinued in 1873.

In 1851 a three-cent piece in silver was issued, and it was extensively circulated until 1887, when it was discontinued. In 1875 a twenty-cent piece was introduced, but it was not popular, and was withdrawn about three years later. The type of the three-cent piece, which was of nickel, was changed several times, and was finally discontinued in 1873.

A so-called trade dollar, authorized in 1873, was quite an innovation, in that it was not intended for circulation in the States, but was minted for use in China, whence it made its way in considerable quantities, until 1887, in which year its issue was discontinued. The type of this remarkably fine coin indicated the commercial purposes for which it was struck; on the obverse Liberty was represented seated on bales of merchandise, her hand, in which was a scroll inscribed "LIBERTY," rested on a sheaf of corn; at her feet was another scroll, on which was written, "IN GOD WE TRUST." On the reverse was the eagle, and on a scroll, "E PLURIBUS UNUM"; in small letters under the motto, "420 grains, 900 fine."

The current coins of the United States scarcely

come within our purview; they are exceedingly well designed, and the later issues represent Liberty in a pleasing form. It is said that when the new coins of recent issue were designed, the artist, being wishful to secure a model of a pure Grecian figure, found her in a waitress in a New York restaurant. Certainly both artist and sitter have contributed towards a successful coinage, the types being uniform in practically all the metals and values of current issues.

Concurrently with the older issues described, the copper cents have chiefly followed the types in use at the time. Very few of them are scarce, except some of the varieties issued before the close of the eighteenth century. All the later issues are obtainable in mint preservation.

SOUTH AMERICAN.

Argentine.

The monetary system of the Argentine Republic is based on that of Spain, of which it was once a dependency. The early coins of gold were, under General Rosa, the Governor, two escudos, doubloon, and rose-doubloon. On these early pieces there is a bust of the general in military dress, the sun being the type of the reverse. During the Republic the doubloon and two escudos pieces were issued.

The early silver of the Republic are of similar types; their values are peso and real, and divisions of the one-peso.

Bolivia.

No gold appears to have been issued in Bolivia for circulation. The silver of 1828, onward, was minted at The Mint, Birmingham, and consisted of one Boliviano and ten, five, and twenty-cent pieces. On most of these is the head of Bolivar: on the reverse are the emblems of the country.

Brazil.

The old coins of Brazil of gold and silver present many attractions to collectors of South American coins. Under Don Pedro I there were gold pieces of the values of moeda d'Ours (4,000 reis) and half-dobra of 6,000 reis ; and under Don Pedro II coins of the same denominations as the last-named were struck. The early silver coins of Brazil were struck under Pedro II, the values ranging from two mil reis to eighty reis. The gold, locally mined, was minted in small quantities ; indeed, the circulation of silver, especially in the middle of the nineteenth century, was small, paper money consisting of Treasury bills and notes of the Brazilian and other banks being mostly used.

Chili.

Rich in metal ores, Chili, soon after it was declared a Republic, in 1817, commenced to issue a new currency. Its gold, which was much below the U.S.A. standard, consisted of the doubloon and its parts. On these, minted about 1839, are the arms and supporters of the Republic ; on some a hand resting on the "book of the Constitution" on the obverse ; on others the date of the founding of the Constitution. The silver consists mostly of pieces of eight reàls and divisions, and five, ten, and twenty-centavo pieces. The volcanic peaks shown on the reverses of some of the coins remind us of the volcanic nature of the country and of the vast destruction eruptions have wrought there. The legend over the emblem is, "CHILE INDENDIENTE," and beneath it "SANTIAGO."

Colombia.

The coins of the early issues of the Republic of Colombia bear the names of the towns of mintage—"BOGOTA" and "POPAYAN"—on their reverses. A somewhat stout female head denotes Liberty, the earliest issues being dated 1827; the values in gold are doubloon and its divisions. On the silver there is an Indian's head, marking the coins of New Granada and Cundinamaca; the emblem on the reverse is a pomegranate, on which is the arms of Granada in Spain; the values are pieces of eight reals and divisions.

Ecuador.

In the early days of the Republic of Ecuador gold doubloons were struck, and silver one-sucre pieces and parts issued. These coins, which were minted at The Mint, Birmingham, are curious and rather misleading to collectors, in that under the arms on the reverse in rather bold letters may be read, "HEATON" (Heaton & Sons, die-sinkers) and "BIRMINGHAM." This issue was followed soon after by silver minted in Quito, the capital of the Republic.

Guatemala.

The gold coins of Guatemala vary considerably in their standard fineness; the largest coin is a quadruple, weighing about 344 grains; of this piece there are parts down to one-sixteenth. The silver is numerous and varied in type, the name of the Republic, however, being always conspicuous.

Mexico.

Mexican dollars mostly exhibit the Cap of Liberty and the Mexican eagle. It was not until 1824 that the power of Spain was broken, and Mexico established a Federal Republic. The gold coins are chiefly doubloons and two and a half, five, and ten pesos. The silver currency is based on the dollar.

There are coins of Honduras, Peru, Uruguay, Venezuela, and New Granada, but they do not call for special mention.

XXI

SEVENTEENTH-CENTURY TOKENS

CHAPTER XXI

SEVENTEENTH-CENTURY TOKENS

Private enterprise supplies small change—Town tokens—Tavern pieces—Traders' tokens.

It is difficult to realize the disturbance to trade made by the Civil War in England in the time of Charles I, resulting in his death and subsequent change of government. Still more difficult is it to grasp the conditions of retail trade in this country in the seventeenth century, when, with more settled conditions and a feeling of security, the countryside once more settled down to the more peaceful arts and crafts, and the implements of war were put away. The somewhat sudden reaction, bringing with it quicker circulation of coin, showed how totally inadequate was the supply of small change, up till then mostly supplied by continental copper ("black money," so called), obsolete abbey pieces, lead tokens, and the small silver coins, many of which had been minted in the Middle Ages. Oliver Cromwell and others at an earlier date had made desultory attempts to improve the condition of the coinage and provide small change. Harrington farthings had been issued under licence during the reigns of James I and Charles I, but they had proved inadequate. There had also been farthing tokens issued by a few traders in London. The lead pieces to which reference has been made had a certain local use, but their circulation was by no means general. These lead pieces, most of which have found their way into collectors' cabinets in a very unsatisfactory condition, were crudely minted.

The emblems used by sixteenth-century traders and by a few at an earlier date were often grotesque, although many of them took their rise from devices which were used as signs by those early shopkeepers, and in some cases formed portions of the arms of the traders' guilds, which were then exercising a powerful influence over manufacture as well as retail distribution in the Metropolis. A very extensive collection of early leaden tokens is now on view in the Guildhall Museum in London, and great efforts have been made to locate the different specimens and to classify them in some kind of order. The devices known as "merchants' marks" for the most part consist of a cross with other lines added, frequently embodying the initial letters of the issuer, sometimes forming an interlaced geometrical design. Among the symbols on such leaden pieces are to be traced birds, anchors, lions, fighting-cocks, boars' heads, a pierced heart, a mason's mallet, and a sugar-loaf. To many collectors of tokens these pieces form an interesting prelude to a more extensive selection of traders' pieces issued in the seventeenth century.

With this miscellaneous coinage in circulation, totally inadequate for the transactions then taking place, traders were faced with the problem of how to carry on their businesses and to give change to their customers. The need was urgent, and the retail traders and innkeepers rose to the occasion. It must be remembered that in the seventeenth century many of the innkeepers were retail tradesmen too, and much business in merchandise was carried on at the inns where traders and travellers resorted. Thus it is that tavern pieces are to be met with in large numbers, supplementing what are usually denominated traders' tokens. Added to these varieties are tokens issued for "the convenience of trade" by town authorities, overseers of the poor, and in some instances by the local shopkeepers, who appear to have formed an agreement together for the joint issue of an acceptable token.

The collection of these seventeenth-century tokens reveals the evolution which has taken place in trade during the last century and a half—since the introduction of steam-power and machinery into mills and works. Once rural districts have become popular centres of trade, and towns which had some importance in the seventeenth century have ceased to exist or have been merged into others. Some few have gone back to the land, and have become little more than agricultural villages. These pieces, so small and easily lost, had inscriptions and emblems in low relief and were often badly struck. Consequently they quickly became rubbed and worn. The varieties, computed to have been some twenty thousand in number, were chiefly of circular form, and were struck out of thin copper sheets or strips, and were minted in small wooden presses worked by a screw. The pieces were issued as they were needed, and although there was a frequent exchange of tokens for the larger silver coins of regal currency, effected by the shopkeepers who issued them on demand, in many places the circulation was general, and often no attempt was made to clear them. In other places greater efforts were made, and the clearing-house system prevailed. Especially was this the case in London, where the changing of tokens became quite a business. At the Tokenhouse, London traders could obtain a fair exchange, or their own tokens in return for those of others. No doubt many of these little pieces were lost, for they were modelled on the type of the Harrington farthings, which were but replicas in copper of the silver half-pennies and pennies of an earlier date. It is said that one of the strong arguments in favour of a much-needed regal currency of copper of larger size was that these little pieces could not be handled by the labourers, whose horny hands could scarcely feel them, and that their loss was a frequent occurrence. The end came in 1672, when by Order of Council it was declared that the issue of unlawful tokens must cease, and the new currency of copper of Charles II which was then ready for circulation must take its place.

The collector has a very definite and short period of seventeenth-century tokens to look out for. The great need for their issue, however, is evidenced to those who search the records and find that one or more tokens, often quite a number of varieties, were issued in almost every town and village in this country during the trade revival after the cessation of war. These interesting pieces are almost invariably distinguishable by the names of the issuers and the places of issue. The reverse usually bears the mark of value, "HIS HALF PENNY," sometimes the issuer's initials are to be seen upon the obverse; at others a trade emblem or the trader's guild arms takes their place, and in the case of town pieces the arms of the town. Tavern pieces are easily recognized by the sign of the inn which generally followed the name of the issuer. On the London tavern pieces there is seldom anything more than the name of the street added; on the provincial tokens, however, the name of the inn and that of the town was sufficient. In many cases it was the sign of the inn, so well known to travellers as well as residents, which acted as a guide-post to the shops of the traders, many of whom placed on their bill-heads the place of their location as being near some noted tavern. The remembrance of this fact will sometimes assist collectors in arranging their seventeenth-century tokens, and in classifying them, for many names of towns and villages are duplicated in other counties often far removed.

Town pieces were designated as such, and appear to have been issued by the local authorities for the convenience of trade, in some cases supplementary to the traders' pieces; in others where the shopkeepers did not supply the needful money for the business then being done—especially in the frequent purchases of small supplies, for which the larger coins of regal mintage would not be suitable. In those days the buying power of money was lessened from that of still earlier times, but it was vastly greater than it is to-day, and the farthing and the half-penny were much in request.

The examples of seventeenth-century tokens which are here illustrated, show that there was great sameness in the circular pieces; as each new issuer ordered dies to be made the die-sinkers followed closely upon the lines adopted in the designs for the earlier pieces which were then in circulation in the neighbourhood. It is evident, however, that there were a few eccentric people in those days, and whether from that cause or with the intention of making their tokens more remarkable than others, and hence, perhaps, of greater advertising value, they struck them square, octagonal, diamond, and even heart-shaped. Referring to the examples indicative of the usual types of circular coins, Fig. 215 is a farthing of Robert Ives, of Whittlesey, in Cambridge; on the obverse is a wool comb, and on the reverse the initials "R.I." The token of Henry Gutch, of Glastonbury, shown in Fig. 216, is an interesting mercer's token; on the obverse is the celebrated Glastonbury thorn, which according to old legend was reputed to have been planted by Joseph of Arimathea, who was supposed to have visited Britain and founded the old abbey. Both the pieces referred to were farthings. The relative sizes of seventeenth-century tokens may be noted by comparing the illustrations Figs. 215 and 216 with the next two illustrations, Figs. 217 and 218, which are half-pennies. John Skidmore, who was a draper

SEVENTEENTH-CENTURY TOKENS.

Fig. 215, Robert Ives; Fig. 216, Henry Gutch; Fig. 217, John Skidmore; Fig. 218, W.R., Cheapside; Fig. 219, Thomas Graymer; Fig. 220, John Halsey; Fig. 221, Roger Gorsuch; Fig. 222, Thomas Farmer; Fig. 223, Nathaniel Poole.

in Rickmansworth, in Hertfordshire, issued the piece illustrated in Fig. 217, in 1666; on the obverse is the maiden's head, the emblem of the Mercers' Guild. The haberdasher's token illustrated in Fig. 218 is of a somewhat scarcer type, for on the obverse is one of the old merchant's marks used by early traders before the adoption of signs hung out over the pavements. This piece was issued from the sign of "The Mermaid," in Cheapside. The square-shaped piece of Thomas Graymer, in Bakewell, shown in Fig. 219, is dated 1669, and is, therefore, a somewhat later type. John Halsey, in Uttoxeter (see Fig. 220), issued a scarce octagonal half-penny, which, like Fig. 217, exhibits the mercers' emblem, as that trader's sign. It is presumed, therefore, that Halsey was a mercer or draper. Another octagonal piece, illustrated in Fig. 222, was struck in 1670 by Thomas Farmer, whose trade is also stated to be that of a mercer, the place of issue being given as Welshpool, in Montgomery; technically described, the arms upon this piece consist of a griffin passant, in chief three lions' heads erased. The old way of spelling the town—Welch Poole—noticeable on all the tokens issued by Welshpool traders, is characteristic of the changes in the names of places. Not only does the spelling of the names of towns vary, but the surnames, and in some cases the Christian names, of the traders seem to have been inscribed and spelt according to the whims or fancies of the die-sinkers or the men themselves. The study of these tokens shows how easily in after-years families drifted apart owing to the methods adopted in spelling their names, for the greater portion of those who handled seventeenth-century tokens were quite illiterate and unable to recognize errors. Dialects and local pronunciation of common words influenced spelling in the same way. Thus we find the concurrent use of "half" and "halfe," and "penny" and "peny."

The next group of tokens illustrated are of rarer forms, for most of the heart-shaped tokens are now scarce. The example given in Fig. 221 is that of Roger Gorsuch, a Liverpool mercer, whose tokens were not issued until 1672. On the obverse of this very interesting and remarkable piece the "babes in the wood" are adopted as the type. It is one of those rare instances of the die-sinker having attempted a picture. Fig. 223 is another heart-shaped token, one issued by Nathaniel Poole, of Macclesfield. It is, of course, a Cheshire token, a county in which very few seventeenth-century traders issued tokens, and nearly all of them are of late date. It is said that the Chester traders refused to comply with the prohibitory proclamation forbidding their use, and two years after its issue, as late as 1674, the tokens were being used in preference to regal coins, and the Government commenced proceedings against the offenders. Chester city was also remarkable in the seventeenth century for the use of penny tokens, of which quite a number were struck, notably by prominent men, among them being Ralph Burroughs, an alderman; Robert Fletcher, sheriff of the county; and William Harvey, mayor.

In concluding this brief review of seventeenth-century tokens, it may be pointed out that an excellent plan is to specialize on one or more counties in which the collector is interested, giving him a good insight into the topography of the district as it was in the seventeenth century. Another specialized collection may be made of town pieces of which many can be gathered, among them being little towns then quite important, but now scarcely known. Such pieces were issued by "THE OVERSEERS OF THE POOR," and others by local "MAYORS."

XXII

EIGHTEENTH CENTURY TOKENS

CHAPTER XXII

EIGHTEENTH-CENTURY TOKENS

Pennies, half-pennies, and farthings—The spirit of the times is seen in the sentiments of the mottoes and inscriptions—Not many farthings of the period.

FOR close on a hundred years after the cessation of seventeenth-century tokens the issues of regal money, especially those struck by George II and George III, were found sufficient to meet the requirements of trade which was as yet very local. Towards the close of the eighteenth century, however, following the discovery and application of steam-power to manufacture, it became evident that copper coins were badly needed. No supply being forthcoming from the Royal Mint, traders as in the previous century took the matter in their own hands, and some of the more adventurous began to strike half-pennies and pennies, the former being the most urgently needed. These coins followed closely the current coinage both in weight and size. Many of them were minted in Birmingham, which was then becoming the centre of an important manufacturing district. In the seventeenth century it was the retail shopkeepers who felt the urgent need of small change. In the eighteenth century, however, manufacturers, who were then employing workpeople on the factory system, found it difficult to procure small change for the payment of wages, and many owners of works and mines put copper tokens into circulation in the weekly payments of wages. In some districts, however, the shopkeepers circulated their own tokens. These pieces were chiefly of good quality, many of attractive designs, types which would be popular in the respective districts in which they circulated, and acceptable substitutes for regal coins.

In most cases the earlier tokens were honest attempts to provide for the convenience of increasing commerce, and to supply the common people with the wherewithal to carry on their trade with the local shopkeepers. The time came, however, when Birmingham manufacturers and speculators found that there was money to be made out of the issue of tokens, especially when there was little or no chance of their being called upon to redeem them. Anonymous pieces were put into circulation, and could scarcely be designated tokens, for their issuers had no intention of their redemption for current coins. The continued apathy of the Government encouraged the issue of freaks, and the dies engraved by some who made a business of preparing and minting such pieces were often outrageous. Together with these tokens which had a fixed nominal value, often only defined by the size of the coin, were discs of metal, which were nothing more than commemorative medals sold by their issuers at a profit. Yet all these nonde-

224

225

226

227

Figs. 224–227, Eighteenth-century Half-penny Tokens.

script pieces passed current, and were accepted in the manufacturing districts in the payment of wages, and by shopkeepers for their relative nominal values, without hesitation.

The possibilities of collecting copper tokens of the eighteenth century are so great that the collector can hardly do otherwise than specialize, and upon some approved principle reject undesirable pieces. The tokens available for selection are pennies, half-pennies, and farthings, but the first and the last-named sizes are comparatively scarce. There is an immense difference in the value of all three sizes of tokens, regulated by their scarcity, but chiefly by their condition. Tokens in other but mint preservation are of quite insignificant value, and the interest in such a collection is lessened materially, and its beauty is marred by the inclusion of rubbed or holed specimens, however scarce they may be. The collector has not only the choice of rarities in circulated coins, but can obtain many of them as bronze proofs, and in some cases gilt. To the ordinary devices there are also rare patterns, which, of course, were not put into general circulation.

The collector having decided upon the method of his selection will naturally aim at making it as representative as possible. As it has been already intimated, most of these tokens were struck during the closing years of the eighteenth century, before that extensive issue of copper made in the year 1797 circulated; for it was, of course, some time before the regal issues of that year reached the more remote country places. The fine series of pennies in mint preservation is well worth attention, for it is not unwieldy, there being entire counties unrepresented, and few towns or villages where more than one or two traders issued pennies. In Cambridgeshire the only dated pieces of that period appear to have been tokens issued in Cambridge, one of quite late date inscribed, "JAMES BURLEIGH'S TOKEN, CAMBRIDGE, 1799." The Macclesfield penny of Charles Rowe is the only one representing Cheshire. There are no eighteenth-century penny tokens of either Cornwall or Devonshire, although several were struck a few years later when a wave of prosperity came to Cornish mines. A Sunderland penny of 1797, on which is illustrated the iron bridge, a notable engineering feat completed in 1796, spanning the River Wear, may be regarded as the sole representative of Durham. Essex is quite unrepresented. A few Gloucester pennies are extant, notably a "City Token" by Kempson. Of these pieces there are several varieties illustrating important buildings in the city. The Netley Abbey "British Penny" of 1797, is an interesting architectural Hampshire token. Batty, in his exhaustive work on tokens, describes a Hereford piece, of 1796, the type of which was a bull, said to be "tossing off its chains." There is a Lancaster penny; with a view of the castle on the obverse, and Lancaster Bridge on the reverse. A scarcer variety of this piece was struck in white metal. Apparently no penny tokens were needed in either Liverpool or Manchester, cities which were then but in their infancy.

In the County of Middlesex, in which London was

228

229

230

231

Figs. 228–231, Eighteenth-century Half-penny Tokens.

then chiefly included, there were comparatively few pennies issued by traders, although there were some speculative issues, and some interesting architectural pieces by Jacobs, Kempson, and others, referred to later in connection with half-penny tokens, were put into circulation. In Norfolk a Lynn corn factor issued a token in 1798; other pieces in the county being issued in Norwich and Yarmouth. At Wroxham in the same county D. Collyer, the proprietor of a marl pit, issued a threepenny piece in copper, which, according to the inscription, was "To pay workmen and to promote agriculture." At Kirby Hall, in Northamptonshire, a curious token, bearing date April 28, 1774, was issued, recording on the reverse the ages of Peter Muilman, aged 68, and Mary Chiswell, aged 61, who, it was said, had "lived in lawful wedlock for forty years." One Mather, an ironmonger, issued a penny in Newcastle-upon-Tyne, in 1797. On the reverse "Justice resting on the emblems of security" is inscribed on a shield, borne by an emblematic figure. Several undated tokens of contemporary date were also circulated. Jacobs's British Penny of 1797, on which is a view of Newstead Abbey, seems to be the sole representative of Nottinghamshire. Jacobs struck a similar piece on which was a view of Sherborne Castle, in Oxfordshire, and another piece showing a building in Dudmaston, in Shropshire, and one of Ludlow Castle in the same county. In Somerset there are penny tokens of Bath, Bristol, and Glastonbury. One very curious and beautifully engraved piece shows a view of the entrance to the Botanic Gardens, of Bath. On it is engraved a quotation: "He spake of trees, from the Cedar tree that is in Lebanon." Another interesting shopkeeper's token of 1794 was issued by Lamb and Son, grocers, of Bath. A Bristol piece is inscribed, "Prosperity to the City of Bristol." The trade of Staffordshire did not call for a local supply of pennies in the eighteenth century, although when a trade boom came in 1811 this county had taken its place as a somewhat prolific centre for the issuing of tokens.

In Suffolk several early tokens were issued in Bungay, and in other towns, notably Bury St. Edmunds. In both Surrey and Sussex several of Jacobs's "British Pennies" circulated. There are a few Warwickshire tokens of the period, and Jacobs issued a penny token in Dudley. Some charming commemorative pieces were struck in Yorkshire, one especially curious penny, on the obverse of which is a view of Bolton Castle, and on the reverse an urn, scythe, hour-glass, and skull, with the legend, "TIME DESTROYS ALL THINGS."

Of Welsh pennies, those issued in Anglesea between 1789 and 1791 are the most important. On all of these the Druid's Head is the type of the obverse. On the reverse, frequently in script, the monogram *P M C* (Parys Mining Company). Collectors of Scotch and Irish coins will find a few pieces dated 1797 and 1798 which may be included in their cabinet.

In addition to the foregoing pieces there are a few provincial tokens on which there are no issuers' names or localities. They are, however, more commemora-

232

233

234

235

Figs. 232–235. Eighteenth-century Half-penny Tokens.

tive in character than *bona-fide* tokens issued for the purposes of trade.

During the closing years of the eighteenth century half-pennies were issued in almost every county in England, and in some few Welsh counties. In some works dealing exhaustively with eighteenth-century tokens the writers have given variations of die, even to faults, as different pieces, going on the principle that, struck from a different die, although the variation might be very trifling, the coin or token could not be identical with others struck from dies which had been broken or discarded. These minor varieties add materially to the collectable pieces of the specialist, but they scarcely appeal to the collector who is interested in tokens as the source of revealing to him historical events occurring in those districts, or indicative of the trade and commerce of the period on which he is specializing. Some tokens are more of the nature of advertising mediums than coins to serve a useful purpose and therefore of little interest. They are not of sufficient purport in their inscriptions to warrant the collector who collects discriminately including them in his cabinet.

The illustrations given here have been chosen to indicate some of the specialistic lines upon which a collection appealing to the direct sympathies of the collector may be formed, for in each section such tokens are widely scattered over the counties. Group A, Figs. 224–227, may be termed architectural, and represents an exceedingly pleasing series which appeals to many. It reminds us in its scope of the beautiful architectural series of Roman coins, which the Emperors caused to be minted to commemorate their great architectural achievements; and it certainly gives those living in the twentieth century an idea of what was then regarded in the eighteenth century as buildings worthy of being commemorated on token currency. Some of those buildings stand to-day; others have perished, or have been rebuilt and modernized. In Fig. 224 a Beccles (Suffolk) half-penny is represented. On the reverse the old bridge over the River Waveney is pictured. The steep pitch of the bridge is observable, also the two lamps by which it was lighted. On the obverse part of the fine old Gothic church in Beccles is shown. No trader's name appears on this piece. Fig. 225 is a token issued by one Heath, an ironmonger, of Bath, who took for the type of the obverse of his token the head of Bladud, the reputed founder of the city, the legend reading, "SUCCESS TO THE BATH WATERS," a view of the pump-room being given on the reverse. Fig. 226 is architecturally interesting in that it gives a view of the old shop-front of Dunham and Yallop, goldsmiths, of Norwich, where this token was issued in 1796. The sign over the doorway is that of a golden eagle. Fig. 227 is a York token, around the edge of which is engraved, "York built A.M. 1223, the Cathedral rebuilt A.D. 1075." There is a view of the Minster on the obverse, and of Clifford's Tower, which was rebuilt A.D. 1100, on the reverse. These few illustrations will serve to show the variety of an architectural series, and how by comparing them the different conditions of industrial

236

237

238

239

Figs. 236–239. Eighteenth-century Half-penny Tokens.

districts and agricultural areas may be ascertained. Such a series is undoubtedly one of the most interesting groups on which the collector can specialize.

The second group B, Figs. 228–231, may be said to be commemorative of persons, and may inspire a collection of personal tokens, around which historic interest centres. The die-sinkers who placed so many anonymous tokens in different localities took advantage not only of the architectural features of the neighbourhood, but of the well-known personalities of people whose names were famous in the particular towns in which they wished to circulate the tokens they had struck. But in addition to the personal tokens issued anonymously, local traders and town authorities took advantage of the popularity of historic names associated with the district, relying on the interest connected with them to ensure a welcome acceptance. Fig. 228 is one of the series struck by James, a noted die-sinker, and is commemorative of John Thelwell, the friend of Lamb and Coleridge, known as "Citizen John." The legend on the reverse which reads, "Truth for my helm, and Justice for my Shield" requires no explanation. Fig. 229 commemorates John Howard, the philanthropist, who died in 1790. Howard's labours on behalf of prisoners, and the success of his appeal to the country's justice, and the subsequent liberation of debtors, is pictured on the reverse of this token. The York half-penny of 1795, illustrated in Fig. 230, carries us back to the days of Constantine the Great. According to legend he was at one time thought to have been born at York, but that story has long been known to be a false one. The issuer of the token illustrated evidently had faith in the legend, for on the obverse is the Emperor's bust with the Roman eagle in his hand, underneath it the inscription, "BORN AT YORK A.D. 271." On the reverse of this piece is the shield of arms of the City of York. There are several other tokens of York City well worth collection. Fig. 231 tells of a great ecclesiastic—Cardinal Wolsey—who was born at Ipswich 1471. This is a trader's piece, issued by John Conder, a draper. Drapers and clothiers were specially notable for the enterprise they showed both in the seventeenth and eighteenth centuries in striking tokens in order to prevent any inconvenience which might arise from shortness of change; and collectors who are interested in this particular trade have ample scope to form a very interesting trade collection.

Enthusiasts over the naval and military glories of this country delight in such tokens as those illustrated in group C, Figs. 232–235. The naval tokens are largely in excess of the military. That is accounted for, perhaps, in that most of the naval seaports were important trading communities, and the call for token currency in times of scarcity of copper would probably be greater in them than in those towns which were military depôts. Fig. 232 tells of the "WOODEN WALLS OF ENGLAND," one of which is pictured thereon. On the obverse is a portrait of Frederick, Duke of York, in the exergue "HALF-PENNY 1795." The edge of the token is inscribed

240

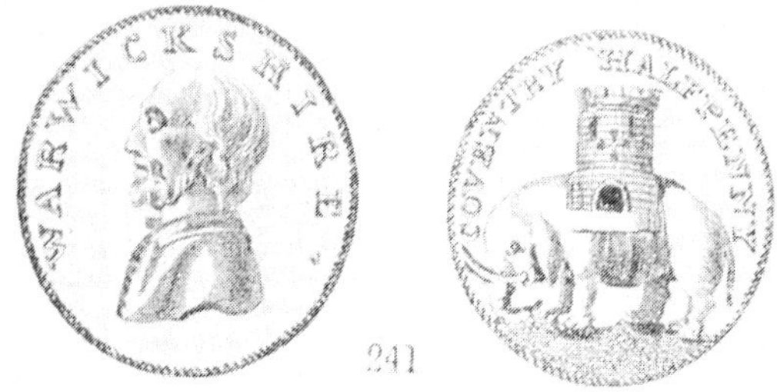

241

242

243

Figs. 240–243. Eighteenth-century Half-penny Tokens.

"PAYABLE AT LONDON OR DUBLIN." Fig. 233 is an Isle of Wight half-penny; on the reverse a galley of the Middle Ages, such an one as is familiar to collectors of mediæval English gold coins. This piece was issued by Robert Bird Wilkins, and was, according to the inscription on the edge, "PAYABLE AT HIS OFFICE NEWPORT." It was an honourably issued trader's token, since the issuer was willing to redeem it in coin of the realm. Another interesting naval piece is shown in Fig. 234; one of the old wooden walls is depicted on the reverse, and the purport of the token is clear from the legend around the vessel which reads, "THE GUARD AND GLORY OF BRITAIN"; on the obverse are the busts of George III and his queen, accompanied by the legend, "LONG MAY THEY REIGN OVER A GRATEFUL PEOPLE." The "GLORIOUS FIRST OF JUNE," the date of the naval victory of Lord Howe, is commemorated on a token issued in 1795, payable by John Skide, of Emsworthy, illustrated in Fig. 235. These are a few typical tokens to which the collector can add both in variety and in places of issue, many of them being obtainable in mint condition.

The next group D, Figs. 236–239, consists of tokens on which are inscribed loyal sentiments, or which in some similar way convey the idea of the loyalty of the issuer to his king and country, and more especially his respect for the Royal House. Fig. 236 represents a popular token of which there were several varieties of obverse, known as the "London and Middlesex Half-penny," according to the inscription round the Royal Arms, on a shield encircled by the Garter on which is inscribed the motto of the Order, supported by the lion and unicorn, and surmounted by the royal crest. Beneath, on a label, is "ICH DIEN" (*I serve*), the motto of the Prince of Wales (afterwards George IV) whose portrait is given on the obverse; the edge inscription on this piece is "PAYABLE AT THE TEMPLE OF THE MUSES"—and evidently it circulated without any intention of redemption. Fig. 237 has for its type Hope, around her the legend "PROSPERITY TO OLD ENGLAND." On the reverse is a sailing vessel. The Hull half-penny struck in 1791 has for its reverse an equestrian figure of William III, in the exergue the date, "MDCLXXXIX," the year of the settlement of the crown on William and Mary (see Fig. 238). This piece, which has the Hull arms on the obverse, was payable at the warehouse of Jonathan Garton & Co. The Biblical injunction, "Render unto Cæsar the things which are Cæsar's," is inscribed on the edge of the handsome token of 1790, illustrated in Fig. 239. On the obverse is a bust of the king by Broz; on the reverse Britannia.

The next series to which attention is called consists of the numerous tokens issued by *bona-fide* traders, who for the most part inscribed their names on the edges. Those shown in group E, Figs. 240–243, are representative of a very large class. Fig. 240 is a Norwich half-penny, which was, according to the inscription on the edge, payable "AT THE SHOP OF DUNHAM & YALLOP." A Coventry token issued

244

245

246

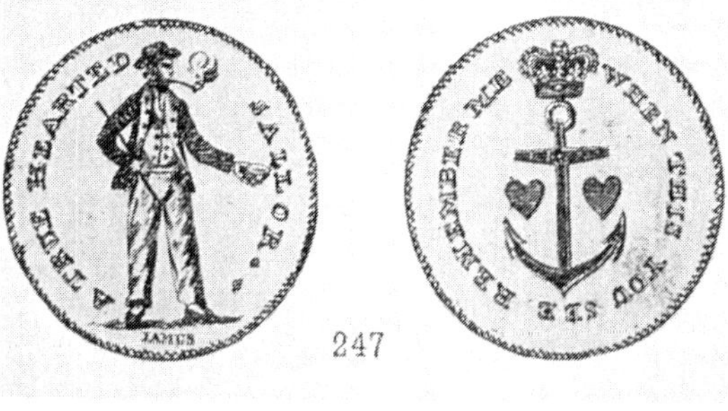

247

Figs. 244–247. Eighteenth-century Half-penny Tokens.

by Robert Reynolds & Co. is shown in Fig. 241, the elephant and castle being the type of the reverse. Another Coventry half-penny issued by the same firm has for the type of the obverse Lady Godiva on horseback, and that of the reverse the allegorical figure of Commerce. This piece is dated 1792 on the obverse, and 1791 on the reverse. The Westminster half-penny of 1792, illustrated in Fig. 243, according to the inscription on the edge, was redeemable at No. 5, Edgbaston Street, Birmingham.

The tokens illustrated in group F, Figs. 244–251, are purely commercial both in their sentiments and inscriptions on their edges. Briefly described, these pieces are a token of Allen & Co., booksellers, who made a bold boast of being the cheapest booksellers in the world (see Fig. 244); Fig. 245 represents a token issued by a London patent cocoa warehouseman, who sold "teas of rough flavour"; Fig. 246 is a half-penny of John Downings, of Huddersfield; and Fig. 247 represents a token issued by Spencer, a noted dealer in coins. The token illustrated in Fig. 248 is a piece of fine die-sinking. Around the device on the reverse there is the commercial sentiment, "Industry, Enterprise, Stability, and Content." "Peace, Plenty, and Liberty" are the sentiments expressed by the issuer of Fig. 249. The trader who circulated the token shown in Fig. 250, a Hereford man, was interested in the success of the cider trade, the intent of his issue of the piece being given on the reverse, "FOR CHANGE NOT FRAUD." A quaint vessel symbolizes the trade of Sandwich on the token illustrated in Fig. 251.

The search for eighteenth-century farthing tokens is disappointing—apparently there was no need for them, or the old farthings of regal issue, and perchance a few of the seventeenth-century trader's pieces served the purpose, even in country districts where small money was mostly in demand. The English eighteenth-century farthing tokens are exceptionally few. The Stowe farthing of 1796 was issued in Buckingham. In Macclesfield there were several varieties representing Cheshire tokens. In Exeter a "half-half-penny" of 1791 was the sole representative of Devonshire trading. Dorset is represented by a Poole farthing of 1795 issued by J. Bayley, a draper. In Essex a "County" token was struck in 1796. In Hampshire farthings were circulated in Portsea and Southampton. Lancashire is almost a blank; among the few, however, are a Liverpool "half-half-penny" of 1791; one of Lancaster; and a Rochdale "half-half-penny."

London does not appear to have been much in need of farthing tokens at that period. Among the few of interest may be mentioned one of Denton, an engraver in Lambeth, dated 1796. Norfolk is represented by a Yarmouth "half-half-penny," of 1792. There is a Bath farthing, which was issued by Lamb & Sons, grocers, who traded at India House, Bath, in 1794, and also by one struck by Heath, a Bath ironmonger, in 1795. In Staffordshire farthings were struck at Lichfield and Stafford. A few were issued in Birmingham, and a somewhat curious piece was circulated in Worcester. In addition to the instances related there are some undated

248

249

250

251

Figs. 248–251, Eighteenth-century Half-penny Tokens.

pieces, and a few which bear dates evidently purely commemorative, and not those of the actual dates of issue.

With the issue of regal copper of all denominations which was minted by Boulton and Watts at Soho Works, Birmingham, in 1797, the need for unauthorized issues ceased for the time. The shortness of the supply of regal coins came again in a different form a few years later, an outline of those irregular issues being given in the following chapter.

XXIII

NINETEENTH-CENTURY TOKENS

CHAPTER XXIII

NINETEENTH-CENTURY TOKENS

Copper pennies and half-pennies—Silver tokens of 1811 and 1812—Countermarked silver—The aim of the numismatist.

THE nineteenth century dawned when England was at war with Napoleon, and for a time trade was at a standstill; in a few years, however, there came a wave of prosperity in the mining and industrial districts, with the inevitable need of small change. In 1811 and following years there were many firms issuing tokens, and it is these pieces, chiefly pennies, which are collectable. Many were really fine pieces, and when in mint preservation are valued additions to the coin and token cabinet; although they do not possess the characteristics which age imparts, and which are such valued attributes in the coins of ancient peoples, or those of mediæval England. These copper tokens were supplemented by silver pieces struck in the years 1811 and 1812. All through the first half of the century, however, there was a desultory issue of "late" pieces, but they are mostly of small interest and were not very generally circulated. Indeed, they were more like advertisements than coins, many being circulated as such by dealers in coins and medals.

Among the most interesting genuine penny tokens struck at the beginning of the century are those issued in Cornwall, bearing such legends as "SUCCESS TO THE CORNISH MINES. 1812." One remarkable piece has a view of St. Michael's Mount, within a circle; another has for its type a fish and pigs of lead, suggestive of the two chief industries of the county—the pilchard fishery and mining. The Devon Mines penny which was issued at Tavistock represents that county. At Stockton-on-Tees a penny was struck in 1813, and appears to have served the district. The owners of the Rolling Mills at Walthamstow, in Essex, issued a penny in 1812, and again another of slightly different type, in 1813.

The Newark penny token was an early piece, having been issued in 1811. Several interesting pennies were circulated in Nottingham, the type generally chosen being a view of the famous old castle in that town. Penny tokens were issued in Bath by S. Guppy, S. Witchurch, and others. There was the ring of honest trading about the legend "ONE POUND FOR 240 TOKENS," appearing on several tokens issued at Bilston, the inscription being accompanied by the name and address of the issuers. The penny tokens of Stafford are of rather unusual dates, having been issued in 1801 and 1803, and really belong to the earlier series; on the obverses are the arms of the borough, and on the reverses a Staffordshire knot. The penny issued by Griffin & Sons, of Withymoor Forge is noteworthy as being dated as late as 1814. A penny token was used at Staverton Cloth Factory, in Wiltshire, in 1811; on the obverse was a view of the factory buildings, and on the reverse a fleece of wool. Several tokens were circulated in Worcestershire, notably one issued jointly by Richard Willis, of Birmingham, and T. and J. Badger, of Dudley. A penny circulated by the owners of the Hull Lead Works, in 1812, was said to be "payable in Bank of England notes by J. K. Pickard." A few traders circulated tokens in Sheffield and district.

There were not many Welsh tokens of the early years of the nineteenth century; among those few may be mentioned a Carmarthen penny, of 1813, inscribed "GLANCLYWEDOG FACTORY. 1813." The Flint Copper Company's tokens of 1811, another from the Flint Lead Works, a Swansea penny, one from Landore, and a penny issued by the Nant-rhydyvilas Air Furnace Company are also of note.

Half-pennies were not so much in demand at the beginning of the nineteenth century as pennies, or if they were the supply of old tokens and the regal copper issued a few years previously was sufficient, at any rate there are few dated half-pennies of this period. Among the more important may be mentioned those struck, along with the pennies, at Walthamstow, by the British Copper Company; the type of which was a lion walking; on the reverse, Britannia, the letters "B.C.C." below. There were a few varied pieces issued by the same Company. A brass token is recorded as having been issued by the "Office of the Leicester Chronicle," in 1810.

A London piece, dated 1814, was payable at Romnanis's in Cheapside; on the reverse was a stocking frame with the legend, "TRUTH, STRENGTH, AND SPEED UNITED." At Norwich, Tunstead and Happing issued a token half-penny in 1812, payable at the Corporation House. Several pieces were issued in Bristol in 1811. There are a few Staffordshire tokens of this period indicating the commercial activity of that district. There is a Stafford county half-penny on which is a bust of George III and the legend, "STAFFORDSHIRE HALF-PENNY TOKEN," on the reverse Commerce is seated with a shield and other attributes, the date is 1814. Samuel Feredy struck a piece at Bilston. Fletcher and Shawatt also issued a Walsall half-penny in 1811, the type being a bear and a ragged staff. A few pieces were added to the Sheffield tokens at this time, but they are not of any great moment.

The silver tokens of Great Britain and Ireland, issued during the years 1811 and 1812 by traders and the Overseers of the Poor, form an independent series, although they were a part of the token currency of the nineteenth century. Many of the series are very poor in design, and by no means minted with care. However, they are of value to the specialist, and many interesting collections have been gathered together. The illustrations which are given in this chapter are a very fair sample of the different types struck by several die-sinkers; one of the most noted being Young and Deakin, of Sheffield. The values were mostly one shilling, and sixpence, although there were some notable exceptions. Fig. 252 is a

252 253 254

255

256 257 258

SHILLING TOKENS:—Fig. 252, W. Horsfall; Fig. 253, Bedworth Mill; Fig. 254, W. Ballans; Fig. 256, S. Sandars; Fig. 257, H. Hunt; Fig. 258, J. Gomme. Fig. 255, GOLD Yorkshire Token.

shilling piece of William Horsfall, of Barnsley; on the obverse is the arms of Leeds, and on the reverse, Commerce. Fig. 253 represents a token payable at Bedworth Mill, issued October 25, 1811, "FOR THE CONVENIENCE OF CHANGE." The Manchester shilling, shown in Fig. 254, was issued by W. Ballans, a tea-dealer in the Market Place; a view of his shop is given on the obverse. Fig. 255 is one of the rare gold tokens of the period. It was for half a guinea, and circulated in Sheffield. The "Gainsbro" token of 1811, shown in Fig. 256, is a shilling issued by S. Sandars; on it may be seen the old bridge over the river. Henry Hunt, of Rowfant House, in Sussex, issued an agricultural shilling on which is a ploughing scene (see Fig. 257). The last illustration, Fig. 258, is a shilling issued by James Gomme, in 1811, at High Wycombe, in Buckinghamshire.

Briefly, mention may be made of the use of foreign coins and tokens made to pass current in this country. The most noticeable of these eccentricities of currency are the Spanish dollars and half-dollars, which, during the long wars between England and Spain and Spanish Dependencies, were captured by British warships, and brought over to England as treasure, generally deposited as bullion in the Bank of England. These dollars, instead of being melted up and recoined, were from time to time countermarked. It is said no less than five million silver coins taken in war were thus countermarked by Boulton and Watt at the Soho Mint, between the years 1797 and 1810, the countermark for the most part taking the form of the bust of George III in a small oval, closely assimilating the mark used by the Goldsmiths' Company for marking plate at that time. There are some scarcer pieces showing the king's bust in an octagon. These Spanish dollars were made to pass current for 4s. 9d., and supplemented the Bank of England and Bank of Ireland tokens already referred to in a previous chapter.

In concluding the story of coins, in so far as it appeals to the average collector, it may be pointed out that to become an expert in any one of the branches of numismatics referred to much patient research is necessary, the minor variations in the inscriptions and legends upon the pieces making all the difference between a great rarity and a piece of quite ordinary value. Moreover, the difference between a coin or token of currency and one of the much rarer pattern pieces may be very slight and scarcely observable to any one unfamiliar with the various types. To become acquainted with these it is desirable to inspect closely, and often, the rare pieces in our museums and in some of the best private collections of specialists. As the cult becomes a specialized study the interest is intensified, and the search after rarities keener. It is the same with every hobby. There is a difference, however, in coins—and stamps—in that mint condition has a more marked influence upon the market value, and also the value in the eyes of an enthusiastic collector, than in the collection of many other *objets d'art* and curios. Age, it is true, lends enchantment, but beauty of condition and the preservation of the piece are what the numismatist seeks; and as the cult is developed in his hands he becomes more fastidious in his choice and in his desire to free his cabinet from undesirable specimens.

BIBLIOGRAPHY

BIBLIOGRAPHY

The books mentioned in the following list refer chiefly to those branches of numismatics treated on in this work:—

Tables of English Silver and Gold Coins. By M. Folks. 1763.

Copper, Silver, and Gold Coins of England. By T. Snelling. 1766.

Nummi Antiqui Familiarum Romanarum. 2 vols. Amsterdam. 1703.

Essays on Medals. 2 vols. By John Pinkerton. London. 1808.

A Numismatic Manual. By J. Yonge Akerman. London. 1840.

Annals of the Coinage of Great Britain and its Dependencies. 6 vols. By R. Ruding. 1840.

Historia Nummorum: A Manual of Greek Numismatics. By Barclay V. Head. London. 1887.

Description Historique des Monnaies Frappées sous l'Empire Roman. 8 vols. By H. Cohen. 1880–92.

Description Générale des Monnaies Byzantines. 2 vols. By J. Sabatier. 1862.

Coins of the Ancient Britons. By J. Evans. London. 1890.

A Dictionary of Roman Coins. By S. M. Stevenson and C. R. Smith. (George Bell & Sons.) London. 1880.

Humphrey's Coin Collector's Manual. 2 vols. (George Bell & Sons.) London.

The Silver Coins of England. By E. Hawkins. London. 1887.

The Gold Coins of England. By R. L. Kenyon. London. 1884.

Greek and Roman Coins. By B. V. Head. London. 1886.

The Copper, Tin, and Bronze Coinage of England. By H. Montagu. (Rollin and Fenardent.) London. 1885.

Guide to the History and Valuation of the Coins of Great Britain and Ireland. By W. S. Thorburn. (L. Upcott Gill.) London. 1898.

Guide to the Department of Coins and Medals at the British Museum. London. 1901.

Encyclopædia of Gold and Silver Coins of the World. By A. M. Smith. Philadelphia. 1886.

The Coin Collector. By W. C. Hazlitt. London. 1896.

Copper Currency of the Canadian Banks. 1837–1857. Ottawa. 1903.

Coins of the Jews. By F. W. Madden. London. 1881.

English Coins and Tokens. By L. Jewitt. London. 1886.

Batty's Copper Coinage of Great Britain. By J. Batty. Manchester. 1868.

Numismata Græca. By L. Anson. London. 1910.

Tradesmen's Tokens of the Eighteenth Century. By J. Atkins. London. 1892.

Coins and Tokens of the British Empire. By J. Atkins. London. 1889.

Nineteenth Century Token Coinage of Great Britain. By W. J. Davis. (J. Davy & Sons.) 1904.

Tokens of the Seventeenth Century in England, Wales, and Ireland. By W. Boyne. (J. Russell Smith.) London.

Silver Tokens of Great Britain and Ireland. By W. Boyne. London. 1866.

London Tradesmen's Tokens in the Beaufoy Collection. By J. H. Burn. London.

Colonial Coins and Tokens. By D. F. Howorth. London. 1890.

English Coins and Tokens. By L. Jewitt. London. 1886.

INDEX

INDEX